William Blake
and Religion

ALSO BY MAGNUS ANKARSJÖ
AND FROM MCFARLAND

William Blake and Gender (2006)

William Blake and Religion
A New Critical View

Magnus Ankarsjö

McFarland & Company, Inc., Publishers
Jefferson, North Carolina, and London

LIBRARY OF CONGRESS CATALOGUING-IN-PUBLICATION DATA

Ankarsjö, Magnus.
   William Blake and religion : a new critical view / Magnus
   Ankarsjö.
       p.   cm.
   Includes bibliographical references and index.

   ISBN 978-0-7864-4559-2
   softcover : 50# alkaline paper ∞

   1. Blake, William, 1757–1827 — Criticism and interpretation.
2. Blake, William, 1757–1827 — Religion.   3. Blake, William,
1757–1827 — Knowledge — New Jerusalem Church.   4. Sex role
in literature.   5. Utopias in literature.   I. Title.
PR4148.R4A8   2009
821'.7 — dc22   2009032014

British Library cataloguing data are available

©2009 Magnus Ankarsjö. All rights reserved

*No part of this book may be reproduced or transmitted in any form
or by any means, electronic or mechanical, including photocopying
or recording, or by any information storage and retrieval system,
without permission in writing from the publisher.*

On the cover: *Beatrice Addressing Dante* watercolor by William
Blake (1824).

Manufactured in the United States of America

McFarland & Company, Inc., Publishers
   Box 611, Jefferson, North Carolina 28640
      www.mcfarlandpub.com

Table of Contents

Acknowledgments
vii

Introduction
1

1. Unitarians, Swedenborgians, Moravians
11

2. Blake's Religion
46

3. Blake's Sexuality
70

4. Blake's Utopian "Colony"
118

Conclusion: "Moravian" Blake
136

Chapter Notes
141

Bibliography
153

Index
159

For my mother and father

Acknowledgments

Like most scholarly work on William Blake, this book has taken a rather long time from inception to realization. When I started collecting material at the British Library in spring 2004 I could not foresee that it would take so many years to complete. But things happen in life, and here we are now several years hence.

On the other hand, for this study I benefited greatly from living and working in the United Kingdom for most of the time. That made access to important material by and on Blake considerably easier, particularly at the British Library, where much of my work was done. There and in other places I gained valuable inspiration from exchange of ideas with various scholars with great knowledge of Blake and his context. And there is little doubt as to who has contributed the most in shaping my book into what it has now become. I am greatly honored to have been working alongside such a knowledgeable and meticulous scholar as my friend and colleague Keri Davies, whose groundbreaking discovery of Blake's mother's Moravian background has forever changed the direction of Blake studies. Thanks are also due here to Marsha Keith Schuchard, who started it all by her sensational finding of Blake's mother in the Moravian archives at Muswell Hill, London. To quite some extent this is the foundation of my book, together with other recent important advances in Blake studies, some of them hopefully my own. My good friend Helen Bruder is the next person that springs to mind here. Apart from her pioneering feminist work on Blake, she gave me warm support in a difficult period. However, I should perhaps foremost send due thanks to Nottingham Trent University for making me a visiting fellow for three years between 2004–2007. The person who brought me to Nottingham was Professor David Worrall, who in his role as research director at NTU continues to inspire scholars of Blake and other subjects. During this project I benefited greatly from ongoing discussions with some of these scholars, so thanks are due to Kevin Hutchings, Tristanne Connolly, Bill Goldman and Will Easton.

Gunilla Florby, professor at my alma mater, Gothenburg University, has always been very helpful with a positive attitude and kindly let me present parts of this project at a seminar. I must also thank Professor Emeritus Morton Paley for his unfailing support and steadfast inspiration. Finally, in the early stages of my project Professor Josephine McQuail gave me congenial encouragement.

But, as always, my warmest thanks go to my partner and colleague Helena Bergmann, without whose love and affection I would not be able to write these lines. There is no doubt that the most important moment in my life came when I met you, Helena. From then on it took a different and much healthier direction. Thank you, my dearest.

Introduction

For almost two centuries William Blake has been considered a Romantic eccentric. This commonplace, standardized conception of him has by now lost contact with all serious scholarship. The commonly accepted view of Blake has even gone so far as to almost assume the anecdotal status of a popular legend. But, through new research and important discoveries, this image can now be thrown in the dustbin. There is little doubt that our image of Blake is undergoing drastic, permanent changes at the moment, embracing the progress of the open-minded scholarship that has become a natural part of Blake studies over the last ten years or so.

Not only must our overall impression of Blake change, but the very details making up this image also must change. In particular, I have in mind recently-much-debated issues like Blake's view of sexuality and his portrayal of women, his potential proto-feminist ideas, his promulgation of a utopian society, and his religious orientation. In all these areas the standard picture of Blake has been contested by a number of scholars in the last few years. It is the argument of this book that the stereotyped image of Blake must be changed even more.

To this end, my book will include documentation of the most crucial discoveries of recent scholarly work. To a large extent the findings and new ideas concern Blake's view of gender, equality, the female and sexuality. The more open-minded interpretation of these issues of the last couple of decades has rubbed off on naturally connected areas. The importance of the way earlier predominantly conservative views of gender and sexuality in Blake, promoted by certain commentators, has been refuted and proved wrong cannot be underestimated. The impact has been pervasive, and today it is not possible to be a serious Blake scholar without bearing these changes in mind.

It is only logical, then, to begin with some words about the shift from the idea of Blake as a sexist person hostile to women to viewing him as one of the most radical voices for equality between the sexes and an avid admirer of women as human and sexual beings. As every Blake scholar knows, an irrevocable paradigm (as it seemed) was set in the early 1980s by two hugely influential articles in the same issue of the *Blake Illustrated Quarterly*, "Blake's Portrayal of Women" by Anne Mellor and "Desire Gratified and Ungratified: William Blake and Sexuality" by Alicia Ostriker. These two essays initiated the mostly negative tone in regard to the impression of Blake's female metaphor, and for quite some time commentators seemed to follow suit, accepting and reiterating the views as a *fait accompli* without bothering to look further into the matter.[1] Admittedly, Ostriker took a more nuanced approach, not seeing Blake's treatment of gender as wholly negative, offering valuable new insights on the way. Unfortunately, in all her subsequent work on the poet, Mellor has persevered in her view of Blake as an irreversible sexist. Basically, she has stuck to her central tenet of "Blake's consistently sexist portrayal of women" (148).

It was not until Helen Bruder's pivotal study, *William Blake and the Daughters of Albion*, appeared in 1997 that this issue took a new and healthier direction. Tristanne Connolly usefully reviews the debate, accentuating the formerly dominant critical divide:

> Gender has been a tortured topic in Blake studies, until recently stymied by the division between critics who see Blake offering an ideal, liberating vision of equality between the sexes, and those who consider that vision to be fundamentally misogynistic [viii].

In my opinion, it is not an exaggeration to say that *William Blake and the Daughters of Albion* is one of the most important books on Blake ever to emerge. It is a pioneering study that has inspired several more daring works, my own included. Possibly the biggest feat of Bruder's book is that not for a minute does she hesitate to take issue with the male-oriented patriarchal tradition of Blake studies. In a long, commendable survey of Blake criticism up to the time of the publication of the book, Bruder scatters praise and rebuttal. She does not try to hide her dislike for the predominantly stagnant and conservative stance of male-centered Blake scholarship, and rightly so. Hence, the most important achievement of Bruder's work is her reading of Blake from a positive feminist position — a first in Blake studies. As Andrew Lincoln puts it:

> Bruder's Blake emerges as a "proto-feminist" influenced by an awareness of Wollstonecraft's observations on the oppression of

women — a view anticipated by some other writers. But the wider issues raised in Bruder's study have yet to be addressed satisfactorily by Blake scholars [231].

Elsewhere, in a distinct way, Bruder has recently expressed her view that Blake "contested so thoroughly the premises of oppressive dominant ideologies that he must be adjudged a radical and prescient sexual thinker" ("Blake and Gender Studies," 135). It is one of the premises of my study that we simply have to concur with Bruder's position here.

William Blake and the Daughters of Albion takes a contextual new historicist approach and investigates Blake's gender utopia in the light of contemporary feminist thinkers such as Mary Wollstonecraft and Mary Hays. According to Bruder, seen in the light of those feminist writers and the sexual politics of the time, one can read Blake as a feminist:

> Blake is of value to feminism not because he maintained an exemplary and unwavering feminist commitment but rather because he took sexual power seriously and engaged with many of the contemporary discourses and contexts in which it was being exercised or resisted [36].

The reception of Bruder's book among Blake scholars has been overwhelmingly positive.[2] This goes to show that it was a much needed work which filled a void in Blake studies. Bruder herself is more modest about her achievement, and in her illuminating essay "Blake and Gender Studies," included in Nicholas Williams's edition of *Palgrave Advances in Blake Studies*, she starts by praising Irene Tayler for kick-starting Blake feminist studies:

> Irene Tayler's "The Woman Scaly" (1973) initiated feminist studies of Blake by confronting head on Blake's troubling concept of "female will," which had habitually been viewed as the essence of Blakean female psychology end either valued as insight or (more rarely) condemned as misogyny. The article broke new ground with the observation that "female will" is not an aspect of essential sexual character but, rather, describes strategies used by the oppressed to gain covert power which are gendered female because women so often find themselves in this position [132].

As Bruder, importantly, goes on, "Her article, then, prepared the way for analysis of his [Blake's] extraordinary insights into the motivated social construction of gender identity and an account of feminist writing after

Tayler shows how this crucial subject forced its way, albeit slowly, up the critical agenda" (132).

However, Bruder's own book seems to have set the stone in motion, and in the wake of her study there have appeared a number of stimulating works on this issue. One of the most convincing studies is Tristanne Connolly's *William Blake and the Body*, which provides another valid commentary on Blake's gender utopia. In this ambitious and competent book Connolly maintains an overall refreshingly positive view of Blake's treatment of gender. However, like most other commentators, she does not perform an altogether positive reading of Blake's female characters and traces some inclusions of sexism throughout Blake's oeuvre. Neither does Connolly see male and female as finally reconciled in Blake's poetry, something which is surely the ultimate crux of the debate over the last few decades, and a major reason for the ensuing critical divide. In spite of all her good ambition, she sees Blake's gender vision as based on male sexual identity, and claims, "I feel disappointed in Blake, because he makes a conscientious effort toward gender inclusiveness, and to a certain extent succeeds, but not completely. He does not go far enough" (xi). But a stimulating, informative and sometimes thought-provoking reading is provided by Connolly's book all the same.

A very special case in the Blake and gender issue, and one which is not possible to place in either of these two main critical strands, is the work of Christopher Hobson.[3] In *Blake and Homosexuality* he argues that several passages in Blake's poems and many of their illustrations have homosexual, even homoerotic, content. It is Hobson's view that by revising his idealization of male heterosexuality, Blake rejects the traditionally anti-homosexual attitude of English radicalism, thus developing a less male-centered idea of gender. He believes that it is fully plausible that Blake advocates an encouragement of sexually deviant expressions. Hobson claims that "Blake's homosexual references, relatively infrequent yet appearing at crucial points in his narratives, constitute [...] a clue to the direction of his thought" (Hobson, xii). Thus, in accordance with his Christian humanism and much in line with his supportive stance of, for instance, women and slaves, Blake expresses support to homosexuals as an oppressed minority. By discussing several examples in Blake, Hobson effectively argues for this position.

Even more crucially, and inextricably linked to these sexual/gender issues, Blake studies of all sorts can now benefit from Keri Davies and

Introduction

Marsha Keith Schuchard's pioneering achievement in establishing the Moravian background of Blake's mother.[4] These discoveries undeniably have a great impact on readings of Blake's ideas on sex, gender and feminism, since the relation between the sexes was one of the key issues for the Moravians, as much as for the other main influence on Blake's religious outlook, the Swedenborgians. It is one of the aims of my book to take advantage of these findings and appropriately apply them to my readings of Blake's poems. Through this I will by example be able to emphasize the need to conform and adjust to the new discoveries.

Briefly put, Keith Schuchard and Davies, with helpful assistance, have recovered and discovered vital information in the records of the Moravian Church archive at Muswell Hill, London. Through an entry in the Marriage Register of the Mayfair Chapel for December 1746, Davies established that the maiden name of Blake's mother was Wright, and that her first marriage was to Thomas Armitage, and not Harmitage, as previously suggested by E. P. Thompson in his influential study *Witness Against the Beast*. By a thorough examination of the Moravian archive, Keri Davies has managed to trace and establish the birthplace of Catherine Wright to the small north Nottinghamshire village of Walkeringham, where she was raised in a family with Moravian beliefs. These new findings rather belatedly complement and verify William Muir's unique nineteenth-century claim, first put forward in Mark Schorer's 1946 study *William Blake: The Politics of Vision*, that Blake's parents attended Moravian services at their Fetter Lane church, before moving on to become adherents to Swedenborg. Until now this crucial claim has been ignored by scholars, with the exception of Schorer who attributes, wrongly as far as we know now, a Moravian influence to Blake's father. So Blake's early religious influences were most likely a mixture of Moravinism, Swedenborgianism and the Church of England, as Schuchard hints:

> Thus, it is possible that the nineteenth-century tradition that Blake learned Swedenborgianism "at his father's knee" is accurate, but it was a Swedenborgianism developed out of earlier Moravian themes ["The 'Secret' and the 'Gift'" 210][5].

The new biographical facts about Blake naturally have urgent implications for the way we read his poetry and interpret his art. For one thing, stemming from a Moravian family meant that equality was a natural everyday ingredient in the Blake household in a way that was not the case for the ordinary Londoner. Equality between the sexes was something that the Moravian church tradition strived for as far as was possible. Schuchard tells us that "their more daring followers experimented with uninhibited sexual behaviour, egalitarian social relations, mystical meditation, and alchemical transmutation" ("The 'Secret' and the 'Gift,'" 211). Quite intriguingly, the most sexually experimental and creative period of the London Moravians, the "Sifting Time" between 1743 and 1753, roughly coincides with the years that Blake's mother Catherine and her first husband Thomas Armitage and possibly her future husband James's brother, John Blake, were at the peak of their activity in the congregation, as Schuchard further indicates: "During the years of the Armitage-Blake attendance, the Moravians participated in Zinzendorf's sexual and spiritual experiments, which produced the most creative and controversial period in the history of their church" (Schuchard, *Mrs Blake*, 31).

Tightly connected to the fact that Blake is of a Moravian family, and also noted by Davies, is the issue of dissent versus conformity with the Church of England. The Moravians were somewhere in-between, or, rather, both. Significantly, this can also be claimed about the Swedenborgians. Hence, to what degree Blake's religious outlook was radical is more uncertain than most commentators have previously believed, and therefore his biography, and his art and poetry, now have to be reassessed. As Davies concludes:

> For Blake scholars, the discovery of the Armitage and Blake documents in the Moravian archives at Muswell Hill opens up a new frontier in Blake studies. The old simplifications will no longer work; modern scholarship of Blake now needs to be repositioned within a very different cultural and religious background ["The Lost Moravian History of William Blake's Family," 25].

Clearly, the dissenting connection, if we still call it that, suggests an unusual acceptance of unorthodox, not traditionally patriarchal Christian, beliefs of greater equality between the sexes. Most crucial, however, is the exceptional open-mindedness that surrounded Blake in his early years, which doubtlessly made him more willing to accept new radical ideas, such as feminism, gender equality and an open-minded attitude to sexuality, at a more mature age.

Blakeans are fully aware of the fact that there is precious little known for certain about Blake's life, so it is after all not altogether surprising that all the many, often quite dubious, stories have become an unluckily

Introduction

cemented part of Blake scholarship, taken for granted for too long and by too many people. It is only with the progressive research in the last ten years or so that this has changed for the better. All these new discoveries contribute to the possibility that Blake studies could take new and healthier turns in the near future. Or, rather, from now on we all must conform to the new, important findings when we write about or teach Blake. There is little doubt that our picture of Blake is undergoing drastic and groundbreaking changes at the moment.

It is my suggestion that the early, twisted conception of Blake has helped to cement other faulty ideas about him. This is an unhealthy position for Blake studies to be in, and it is no great surprise that a number of long-lived critical fallacies have been created ever since Blake entered the academic world with the help of T. S. Eliot, in the wake of Yeats, Ellis and S. Foster Damon's pioneering work at the beginning of the twentieth century. Robert Rix makes a similar assumption in the conclusion of his recent often useful study *William Blake and the Cultures of Radical Christianity*, which mainly centers on Blake's relation to Swedenborgianism:

> [T]he nature and direction of Blake's art is best understood in relation to particular cultures of dissenting or radical Christianity. Blake's ideas belonged to certain cultural traditions and religious strands which have not survived well into modern times. Perhaps for this reason, they have inhabited only the fringes of scholarly interest [155].

The most serious misinterpretation of Blake was in fact established less than two decades ago by a famous and important contemporary commentator, namely the great historian E. P. Thompson. In his widely acclaimed 1992 study *Witness Against the Beast*, he most alluringly argued that Blake was raised in a Muggletonian family and environment. This has now been convincingly proved wrong by the discoveries by Keri Davies and Marsha Keith Schuchard that Blake's mother was of Moravian background and was a devoted and active member of the Fetter Lane society of this church.[6] Nonetheless, people still tend to take Thompson's scholarly authority as a guarantee for the correctness of the Muggletonian argument and, recently, I have myself come across a couple of academic colleagues knowledgeable about Blake, who refer to this as being the latest important fact about him. With obvious fascination they have referred to Thompson's study as one of great interest and importance. I agree that *Witness* in many ways is still an interesting book, but unfortunately its main argument is completely wrong. I also have to agree that the study is still of some importance since it was Thompson who discovered that Blake's mother had been married once before she married James Blake. So we have to give Thompson this credit; he was in fact the one to put Davies and Schuchard on the right track. Unfortunately this does not make the Muggletonian argument any less incorrect, and it is now high time that we stop referring to it. Blake was not raised a Muggletonian — he was a Moravian.

We must also interrogate the meaning and the connotations of the (perhaps too) commonly used term "radical." This term is used somewhat vaguely, sloppily and even carelessly and this may naturally lead to all sorts of premises and conclusions — not least with such a unique artist and personality as William Blake. When discussing and analyzing Blake and his works we must make clear that we use words like "radical" in their correct, or at least commonly defined, understanding. Hence, we must ask ourselves, can we label the Moravians radical? Can we call Swedenborg and his followers radical? Can we use the term for any other person or group of people in Blake's immediate environment, for instance the familiar circle of artists and intellectuals around the publisher and bookseller Joseph Johnson? Was Blake's friend, the "first" feminist, Mary Wollstonecraft, radical? It is my hope that through the discussion in this book the issue of radicalism shall at least become clearer.[7]

These important matters will be thoroughly discussed in my book. I will begin by outlining the historical background of the Moravians and the Swedenborgians, and also the Unitarians, since this was the largest nonconformist congregation at that time and, more significantly, many of the people that Blake socialized with in the most radical and formative years in the 1780s and 90s belonged to this creed. In the first chapter dealing with Blake I will assess his poetic oeuvre in the light of the new discoveries pertaining to religious ideas and symbols. The emphasis will be on poems hitherto often neglected by critics, such as the *Notebook* poems and *The Pickering Manuscript*. I will then move on in the next chapter to apply what has been discussed above to the theme of sexuality, with the same preference to rarely discussed poems. Sex and religion must be considered cornerstones of Blake's art and poetry, and are used to create his ultimate vision of a utopian society and existence. In the main, this is a figment of the imagination, so to speak, and as we know, to Blake all reality is mental, but for at least one short period of his life this took practical proportions in the form of a Swedenborgian colonial venture, which had the slave-trade as one significant component. This will be the subject of my fourth chapter. Finally, I will conclude by looking into the future of Blake studies, indicating roads still not taken.

Unitarians, Swedenborgians, Moravians

For more than a decade, ever since the publication of E. P. Thompson's speculative study *Witness Against the Beast* in 1993, followers of Blake were led to believe that Blake was born into and raised in a Muggletonian family. In spite of the lack of concrete evidence other than the Great East Cheap signatures of William Blake and his wife Catherine, this false argument has been spread and perpetuated to a wide audience. However, thanks to groundbreaking research in the last few years, we can now be next to certain that the creed of Lodowicke Muggleton exerted no influence on Blake. The influence is much more likely to have come from contemporary Unitarians, Swedenborgians and, particularly, Moravians—three dissenting religious orientations with some major ideas in common.

It is clear that the dissenters and nonconformists extended a major influence on the Romantic period, as Daniel White confirms: "The religious dispositions, political aspirations, economic interests, and literary tastes of Dissenting communities impelled the genesis of Romanticism in England" (1). In relation to Blake, however, it is difficult to decide which term, if any, to use: dissent, non-conformism or antinomianism. As Robert Rix puts it in *William Blake and the Cultures of Radical Christianity*: "His writing ... presents a determined anti-legalism, rejecting laws and orthodox morality, which may classify as antinomianism — albeit this is a name of opprobrium to which neither Blake nor other believers of similar beliefs would confess" (7). Dissent and non-conformism are to quite some extent debatable terms. Daniel White makes a worthwhile attempt at a distinction in his recent study *Early Romanticism and Religious Dissent*: "I use the term 'nonconformist' to describe a range of religious beliefs and dispositions that prevented English Protestants from conforming to the Articles and rites of the Church of England. By 'Dissent' I mean the three principal denominations of 'Old Dissent'—the Presbyterians, Independents (or Congregationalists), and Baptists—as well as the Unitarians," who evolved out of Old Dissent (188n2). In the main I will follow White's definitions, but with the Swedenborgians and the Moravians this will prove difficult. This is particularly the case with the Moravians and their unique relation to the Church of England and other state churches, a connection which will be explained more thoroughly a bit further on in my text. Quite logically, the Moravians are not included in White's book and, interestingly, he also states that "[a]lthough William Blake ... could be treated in this manner, [he is a] less obvious candidate" (2). Very surprisingly, *An Oxford Companion to the Romantic Age* does not include any definition at all of the term "dissent." On the other hand, it includes an entry on "Anglicanism," which was the religious faith of the majority of the English and Welsh people during this period. It is much easier to find a clear-cut definition of "dissent" in eighteenth-century dictionaries. A relevant example can be found in the famous dictionary of Dr. Johnson: "Dissent'er, s. one who dissents from, or does not conform to the ceremonies of the established church" (Hamilton, *Johnson's Dictionary*, 65).

The Church of England was established as the national church in The Act of Uniformity of 1662. The act also established a distinct category of Christian believers who wished to remain outside the national church and became known as non-conformists or dissenters. All dissenting places of worship—rooms, houses or chapels—had to be registered with the Bishop of the Diocese, the Archdeacon, or the Justices. Under the 1689 Toleration Act dissenters had to swear allegiance and supremacy and subscribe to the declaration against popery. Dissenting "teachers" had to "qualify" by subscribing to the Thirty-Nine Articles, excepting articles 34, "Of the Traditions of the Church," 35, "Of the Homilies," and 36, "Of Consecration of Bishops and Ministers," and certain words of article 20, "Of the Authority of the Church" (and, in the case of Baptists, of article 27, "Of Baptism"). In order to avoid harassment by the authorities and obtain some protection against the mob, registration was necessary, but it was also an admission of dissent from the Church of England.[1]

Another term that Rix makes frequent use of throughout his study is "enthusiasm," which denotes "the belief in divine inspiration," whereas "antinomianism" is "the denial of all other authority than that of the spirit" (3). While Rix is keen to apply the enthusiasm label to Blake, and also taking into account Jon Mee's two influential studies *Dangerous Enthusi-*

asm and *Romanticism, Enthusiasm, and Regulation*, I find it more doubtful that Blake made any widespread conscious use of the term, in spite of a few occurrences of it in his poetry.[2]

Particularly complex is the relation to the Church of England regarding the Moravians, as we shall see further on. Rix offers a helpful initial outline as an introduction to the unique standing of the Moravian Church in Blake's time:

> Moravianism played a key-role in preparing the ground for an awakening of a religion of the heart in England, which was seen to combat the lethargic and complacent attitude of the eighteenth-century Church. The Moravian movement was instrumental in what has come to be known under a broad definitional canopy of Evangelicalism, a term covering a number of reformist tendencies both in and outside the Church of England [8].

Rix then goes on to state, quite rightly, that "[t]he influence of this wider religious development on Blake's writing is undeniable" (8). More debatable is his claim that "Blake's writings show no tell-tale signs of the more distinctive traits of Moravian practice" (8). This is not quite correct, as we shall shortly see.

The Muggletonian Issue

As is familiar to most Blake scholars, in *Witness Against the Beast* E. P. Thompson presents the argument that Blake was born and raised in a family adhering to the ideas of the Muggletonian doctrine. He argued that the little, obscure sect of the Muggletonians exerted the greatest influence on Blake. This is the main argument of *Witness Against the Beast,* and he invests considerable effort in tracing the possible Muggletonian influence of Blake's family. In his discussion, Thompson emphasizes features which point to similarities with Blake, such as the typical Muggletonian vocabulary of symbolism, the belief in a singular God or Christ in the image of man, the embracing of certain feminist principles through an unusually active feminine presence, which of course could have pointed to Blake's belief in an active female. However attractive and tempting it might be to apply these to Blake, it is not very likely that he had any knowledge of Muggletonianism.

Even though Thompson managed to demonstrate some similarity between the Muggletonians and the Swedenborgians, in Blake's case this is almost certainly only a coincidence. As is well known to Blakeans by now, Keri Davies has succeeded in proving Thompson's theories wrong by discovering that Blake's mother was of a Moravian family and not, as Thompson believed, of Muggletonian origin. As we also know, the reason behind Thompson's unsuccessful speculations was a confusion of the name of the first husband of Blake's mother. Davies has presented evidence that his name was Thomas Armitage, and not Hermitage/Harmitage, as Thompson wrongly assumed.[3] Nevertheless, Thompson's book provides interesting reading which still has value in that it points to a non-conformist connection of Blake and his family in a tradition other than the Church of England. Thompson, as mentioned, also was the one who discovered that Blake's mother Catherine was married once before she married Blake's father-to-be.[4]

Unitarianism

"In the late eighteenth century Unitarians were leaders in promoting religious, political and social change" (33), writes Ruth Watts. Indeed, the Unitarians were by far the biggest in number and in many respects the dominant dissenting or nonconformist congregation at that time. Particularly it seems that a large number of prominent radical people were associated with the Unitarians, and several of these were part of the circles that William Blake socialized with. One such group that included an unusually large number of Unitarians was the much-discussed coterie around the publisher and Blake's sometime-employer Joseph Johnson. The impact of this Unitarian milieu has mainly been overlooked by commentators on Blake, but an exception is found in the essay "Blake and the Bible" by Stephen Prickett and Christopher Strathman:

> As a member of Joseph Johnson's circle, which included Godwin, Mary Wollstonecraft, Paine, Priestley, Holcroft, and Price, he [Blake] was in touch with the Unitarians— virtually the only group in England to know of the new Biblical scholarship, which had as yet, made few inroads into a country still isolated [111–12].

By pointing out these important intellectuals as downright Unitarians, the two authors indicate the existence of such ideas in Blake's naturally radical environment. While it is not the purpose of my study to prove any clear Unitarian influence in Blake's art and poetry, I believe it would be a mistake to neglect the constant presence in the 1780s and 90s of such thinking in Blake's vicinity. While he would not condone the rather rational basic features of Unitarianism, Blake could at least take a stand against what he did not like. Particularly, the strong Unitarianism of Joseph Johnson could be of greater importance than has previously been recognized. What if the difference in religious propensity between Blake and his "publisher" gave rise to heated debates, and even discord, which made Johnson a bit cautious to print and promote Blake's material? Perhaps Blake's art and poetry was too radical even for a man like Johnson? We have an intimation of this in *The French Revolution* project, which was abandoned after only one of a proposed seven parts was printed by Johnson. In the end nothing of the poem was ever properly published.

The overall size and importance of the Unitarians, however, is a matter of debate. While some commentators downplay their impact, there are those who consider them to have been neglected by critics.[5] Kathryn Gleadle, for instance, claims that "[t]he immense influence which this denomination exerted upon contemporary culture has rarely been fully acknowledged by historians" (8). Their size also much depends upon whether you count predecessors such as Presbyterians, Socinians and Arians in among the Unitarians or regard them as separate congregations.

In 1791 the Unitarian Society for Promoting Christian Knowledge was established, with Joseph Priestley as one of its founder-members. Even though Unitarianism came strongly to the fore only in the nineteenth century, it had its origin in the preceding century. "Though Unitarian theology became increasingly prevalent among English Presbyterians, Unitarianism did not become a separate denomination until the nineteenth century," Stuart Andrews explains. He continues to state that in the latter part of the previous century "it was still merely a theological tendency" (3). It was at that time that a confluence of Arian and Socinian believers formed the English Presbyterians. Even though other non-conformist groups helped to form the Unitarians, the Presbyterians were their direct forerunners, and most commentators in the field see a direct lineage between the two. Importantly, considering the relatively big following of Unitarianism, Presbyterians made up half of the community of non-conformists at this point in time.

Unitarians took their basic philosophic ideas from John Locke, with important support from his foremost successor David Hartley. Unitarianism was a religion for intellectuals, and therefore they put great value in the ideas of their philosophical forefathers. Public duty was very important to them, with particular emphasis on moral and intellectual education. Their educational work was quite progressive and they were involved in the founding of London University. Through the lead of Mary Wollstonecraft and others, there was an uncommonly strong focus on female education and on making education equal for both genders. As a whole, Unitarianism was very concerned with gender issues and played an important part in the emerging feminist movement. "Their key beliefs enabled Unitarians to hold a much higher conception of womanhood than was generally prevalent," Watts writes, and continues: "Their rejection of both original sin and the essential depravity of man — the blame for which was usually shifted onto woman's shoulders— gave them a fresh, more generous view of the humanity and possible perfection of all" (77–8).

Unitarianism was a fashionable religion among literary people. It was centered around Stoke Newington, with the Aikin and Barbauld families as its most prominent figures. Mary Wollstonecraft was another famous Unitarian, just like her friend, the author and journalist Mary Hays. Significantly, Hays's long-time love William Frend, one of the foremost Unitarians, also lived at Stoke Newington. Other well-known Unitarians were Samuel Taylor Coleridge, the distinguished essayist William Hazlitt and the diarist Henry Crabb Robinson.

The Unitarians were faithful to the interpretations of the Bible, and they believed that God had laid down the laws that governed the universe. Another cornerstone of Unitarian ideology was individualism. While this fits well with what we know of William Blake, there was one item on the Unitarian agenda that was not easily reconciled with his views, namely its early great focus on materialism. This was appropriately combined with its liberal political outlook and resulted in many successful manufacturers among the Unitarians. In the late eighteenth century more radical tendencies in society came to influence the Unitarians, for instance the legacy of the French Revolution in the 1790s. Gradually, radical ideas came to have a greater impact on Unitarianism and, according to several commentators, in the 1820s and 1830s it became appropriate to talk about "Radical Unitarianism." By then the Unitarians had a good number of contacts with different left-wing movements.

One such group of great importance was the early feminists. "Given the progressive nature of Unitarianism, it is perhaps not surprising that Unitarians were often sympathetic to advanced ideas of womanhood," as

Gleadle puts it (21). The major impetus of course came from Mary Wollstonecraft, who was closely involved with the movement. Other prominent Unitarians like Anna Barbauld, Mary Hays and William Frend then cooperated and developed her radical beliefs. "William Frend and George Dyer encouraged Mary and Elizabeth Hays, fervent disciples of Wollstonecraft already, to write on women's rights," Watts informs us (93). Through this, many Unitarians became aware of the radicalism of women's rights, thus creating a sympathetic environment for the growth of feminist awareness. One of the fields benefiting from this was progressive education, much in line with Wollstonecraft's Rousseauan views of a furthering of the education of young people.[6]

The foremost expression of the Unitarian attitude to feminism was its striving to improve gender relations with greater equality between the sexes in mind. This is certainly a feature that fits well into Blake's utopian scheme with complete gender equality as its aim. The Unitarians did not believe that society did enough to meet the demands for better personal opportunities for women and therefore actively sought to rectify this deficit. Particularly, this was the view of many Unitarian women. In *Gender, Power and the Unitarians in England 1760–1860*, Ruth Watts claims "that Unitarians played a significant role in changing ideas on women's abilities and what they could do" (1). Emphasizing this new, improved and more liberal female position, Mary Hays, in her epistolary novel *Memoirs of Emma Courtney*, writes that "from exercising my thoughts with freedom, I seemed to acquire new strength and dignity of character" (40). However, the opinions of society in general were rather skeptical about women and their aptitude for education, as Watts indicates in her comments on *Emma Courtney*: "Her passionate outpourings were too radical for the times but they were indicative of the willingness of these radicals to explore new, and to many outrageous, ideas" (93). The attitude of the Unitarians was much more optimistic about equal opportunities for men and women, as Ruth Watts makes clear: "The two Unitarians, Priestley and Hays, though of different sexes, had similar attitudes towards women" (14). Indeed, Priestley himself wrote: "Certainly, the minds of women are capable of the same improvement and the same furniture as those of men" ("Reflections on Death" 419, in Watts 36).

Priestley is a monumental figure in the Unitarian context — "the great explicator of modern Unitarianism," in the words of Kathryn Gleadle (10) — and also for Blake he was of importance with the meetings at Joseph Johnson's bookshop as a mutual forum for the exchange of ideas. How frequently they actually met remains, like so much of the Blake biography, something of speculation. But we do have Alexander Gilchrist's next-to-first-hand account of the regular participants of the Johnson group, and here both Blake and Priestley are included (*The Life of William Blake*, 79).

The proximity of the two becomes more likely, I believe, if we consider two important factors. Firstly, the ideological sympathies of the other persons in, or in close connection with, the Johnson circle. Of all dissenting groups, the Johnson bookshop seems to have been specifically important to the Unitarians: "His shop and home in St Paul's Churchyard became one of their favourite meeting places," Watts states (91). Secondly, some not frequently discussed striking similarities of the artistic ideals of Blake and the more down-to-earth philosophy of Joseph Priestley must also be taken into account.

The Unitarian creed was, after all, wider and more general in scope than the more esoteric sects such as the Swedenborgians, the Moravians, the Ranters, or the Muggletonians, and it is therefore not surprising that it attracted more adherents. Logically, that also goes for the Johnson group where, besides Priestley, Hays, Wollstonecraft, William Godwin and, most importantly, Joseph Johnson himself, all were Unitarian supporters to various degrees.

At first inspection, though, there might be more that keeps Priestley and Blake apart than unites them. The major discordance is of course Priestley's and the Unitarians' great reliance on the faculty of reason and rationalism as the foundation for their entire doctrine. Their position has come to stamp the label "rational Dissent" on Unitarianism. Given what we know about Blake's staunch opposition to the Urizenic science of reason of Newton and Locke, for instance, it is easy to write Blake off as unsympathetic to, and irreconcilable with, Priestley's views. But if we keep Blake's basic dualist/dialectic strategy of his artistic production in mind, the incompatibility of their positions becomes less obvious. In fact, Blake nowhere advocates an elimination of reason from the general thinking of man. As with everything in Blake it needs to be evenly balanced, in this case with what we may call the faculty of imagination. Man needs both of these faculties, which Blake has made clear in *The Marriage of Heaven and Hell*, for example. Blake's argument is rather that in the dogmas of certain Enlightenment philosophers reason came to be overly predominant, something which he opposed.

This is of course not to say that Blake ever advocates a predominant use of reason throughout his poetry, and there certainly are more self-evident points of agreement between him and Priestley than this. The belief in the individual is one such common feature. It may be significant that the only reference to Joseph Priestley in Blake's poetry is a negative one which clearly alludes to the rational use of the faculty of reason, indicated by the inclusion of Blake's frequently mentioned "arch-enemies" Francis Bacon and John Newton. In this example Priestley, a bit surprisingly, substitutes for John Locke, who is the one nearly exclusively used elsewhere in this triad: "Like dr. Priestley & Bacon & Newton" (E 39).[7]

Although it is a contested point, it is probably in the field of religion that the two men shared the most common ground to make for a fruitful, and probably heated, discussion. After all, Unitarianism was a radical religion in an age dominated by the British government's continuous systematic repression of all dissenting congregations. The emergence and rapid growth of the Unitarians was important because of its capability for general public attraction at a crucial point of time for religious freedom in Britain. However, the inclusion here of a more rational belief in Priestley's religious outlook also speaks against a more unanimous view of the two men.

Both the religion of the Unitarians and that of Blake were progressive. Unitarianism was radical in many of its basic tenets and most formative was its staunch opposition to all that state religion represented. To contradict the opposition of state religion, the Unitarians promulgated a progressive reformation of corrupt religion. We know how Blake, throughout his writing, unfalteringly condemns all institutionalized religion, which he varyingly calls Natural or Sexual Religion. But, however radical otherwise, the religious opinions of Priestley were always essentially of a reactionary nature.

Unitarianism was a philosophy reliant on history. Unitarians used a sophisticated rational historical method, and must be regarded as important historical Biblical critics. For one thing, Priestley proved the falsehood of Biblical doctrines, in regards to the Trinity and the divinity of Christ. They believed in a progressive movement of history towards perfection. This seems to be a utopian tendency which has its equivalent in Blake's prophetic utopian poems, in which he describes a progressive movement towards apocalypse and utopia. Also Priestley has been conscribed with a utopian inclination.

While the Unitarians did not acknowledge the divinity of Christ, they had great faith in the humanity of Christ as a person. This specific view of Christ both goes against Blake's belief and conforms to it. Blake, of course, stresses the divinity of both Christ and man. On the other hand, we know how Blake emphasizes a Christian humanist ideal in his later poetry, most powerfully in *Jerusalem*, with the Brotherhood of Jesus and the forgiveness of sins as a major concept.

Another major talking-point for Blake and Priestley may have been language, and, more specifically, the issue of how mankind can develop existing languages in order to express new phenomena and psychological entities and states of mind hitherto unaccounted for. The extremely versatile Priestley also worked as a linguist and published several books in the field. Priestley had an idea to create new languages, which to some extent we have to give Blake credit for successfully doing with his own unique mythological system in the prophetic books, with their many characters with exceptional and exotic names.

Moreover, the publishing industry was important to the Unitarians in order for them to circulate their often radical ideas to as great a number of the public as possible. Therefore, it was only natural that many of them were linked to Joseph Johnson's printing-shop. Johnson, famously, was the publisher of all Mary Wollstonecraft's work, but there were other emerging presses at that time, as Ruth Watts points out: "It was indeed through their writings that Unitarians sought to disseminate their educational philosophy. The establishment of William Eyres' printing press in Warrington stimulated many tutors to publish their work" (51).

Swedenborgianism

It is striking that the three non-conformist orientations discussed here in their early stages all relied on one charismatic and dominant leading personality. The Unitarians had their Priestley and the Moravians had their Zinzendorf, but for no dissenting group is this as obvious as with the Swedenborgians. The omnipresence of Emanuel Swedenborg in the works, records, teachings and manifestations of this congregation is nearly all-inclusive. And quite naturally so, since unlike the other denominations its creed is based on one person's documented spiritual experiences. It even bears his name.

Significantly, being himself in the same vein of multitalented renaissance men, Joseph Priestley referred to the great Swedish mystic as Baron Swedenborg, or as *"the grand man"* (*Letters to the Members of the New Jerusalem Church*, 55, italics in original). These characterizations serve as useful descriptions of the illustrious past and the unique versatility of the man. Being of noble Swedish origin and the son of a bishop, to modern eyes it looks as if Swedenborg for some time had a part of every important office in his native country. To his original profession as an engineer in the mining industry, where he became an overseer and finally Minister of the Swedish mines, he also was a natural scientist and a member of the Swedish Parliament. While this points to an impressively wide-ranging mind and capacity, it can at the same deter potential interest in his writings, as Ariel Hessayon indicates:

> Swedenborg's voluminous output ranging from treatises on mathematics, longitude, anatomy, physiology, chemistry, cosmology, geology, metallurgy, mineralogy, philosophy and theology to journals recording his dreams and spiritual experiences, coupled with his inaccessible style — even in translation — has tended to discourage all but the committed specialist reader [19].

Initially, Priestley was quite positive towards Swedenborg and saw many mutual points between Unitarianism and Swedenborgianism, even though the two churches to some extent were competing for politically radically inclined members. Common points stressed by Priestley in his *Letters to the Members of the New Jerusalem Church* were a figurative understanding of the Bible with an anticipation of a spiritual millennium and the rejection of the Trinity, original sin and Calvinism. Both Priestley and Swedenborg were looking forward to the time when mankind would be liberated from Christian corruption and religious oppression (Rix, 72).[8] Obviously, most of these points are ones that Blake eagerly subscribes to as well.

But Priestley was not wholly positive about Swedenborg. He was, in fact, skeptical about some of the characteristics of Swedenborg as a person and about certain major features of Swedenborgianism. Most of all, this is obvious in his *Letters to the Members of the New Jerusalem Church*, written two years after Swedenborgianism's formation at the East Cheap convention in 1789. The occasion that inspired Priestley to write these letters was the Swedenborgian opening of an "elegant place of worship" in Birmingham in June 1791, when they claimed themselves to be Unitarians. Priestley thought their faith was too extreme and completely devoid of reason:

> To many persons it will appear not a little extraordinary, that a scheme of religion so visionary, and so destitute of all rational *evidence*, as that of Baron Swedenborg, should be so firmly believed by such numbers of persons of unquestionable good sense, and the most upright intentions; and some may be disposed to say that christianity itself might have had no better an origin [Priestley, *Letters*, xii].

In contrast to Swedenborg, Priestley was not a visionary. After all, his major professional background was as a natural scientist and he is chiefly famous for being one of the discoverers of oxygen. Thus lacking the Unitarians' founding principle of rationality, Priestley was able to criticize Swedenborgianism as a system. Swedenborg's system differed so much from other faiths, that it required proportionally strong evidence. This evidence Priestley found missing: "His system failed to simplify the idea of God, gave no closer access to God, and rivalled the Catholics for lack of tolerance" (*Discourses on the Evidence of Revealed Religion*, 214). More surprisingly, Priestley believed that since their faith lacked miracles, Swedenborg could not be a messenger from God (*Letters*, 54–55).

And that was, after all, something of what Swedenborg claimed: that he, from the time that his visions of the spiritual world began in autumn 1743, had made regular visits to heaven and spoke daily with angels. Maybe it is just a matter of use of terminology, but to make such visits and to speak with angels surely is if not downright revelation something of a miracle. It is of course here that Swedenborgianism so easily and, to detractors like Priestley, obligingly, lends itself to skepticism. We can never know for certain, but probably this was a major reason why Blake's initial enthusiasm cooled off considerably and gradually, until in later years he found another way to better appropriate and accommodate Swedenborg's ideas. Perhaps this was also a point of disagreement in discussions between Blake and Priestley.

Neither would Blake have appreciated the quickly growing conservatism of the Swedenborgian circles in London. While the Church started out in a radical way and exerted a great attraction to all sorts of liberals, dissenters, anti-clerics and republicans,[9] it soon turned much the opposite way to become quite conservative. One major source of this was the conversion of the previously radical Robert Hindmarsh, who was a leading figure in the Church at the time of the inaugural East Cheap conference. Shortly after this meeting there was internal strife within the Church about sexual politics and Hindmarsh was expelled together with five others.[10] Hindmarsh, however, was soon to make a comeback as a now conservative leader, and through the launch of *The New Jerusalem Journal,* of which he was the single editor for two years, he managed to promote his new creed and considerably change the political course of The New Jerusalem Church in a remarkably short spell of time. Whatever the overall social and political pressures were on Hindmarsh for this drastic conversion, we know that it rhymed well with the post–French Revolution conservative backlash. Certainly, this must have been a major reason for the swift distancing of Blake from the Swedenborgians. Indeed, one can subscribe to Robert Rix's pertinent question: "Was Blake part of a group of believers driven out, as the clerics in the New Jerusalem Church embarked on a conservative course?" (127). And significantly, this was starting to take place already at the time of Blake's short immersion with them, as Rix points out: "Already around the time Blake was in contact with the Swedenborgians, there was a move towards ridding the Church of its radical associations" (82). On the other hand, Rix suggests another more debatable reason for Blake's likely severing of the links to the New Jerusalem Church around the time of the first general conference at East Cheap or shortly after. In the context of faith healing and the then widespread practice of animal magnetism and visionary hypnosis as a form of therapy, Rix offers the argument that the fact that the prohibition of such practices for any individual Swedenborgian would be a sacrilege against the Swedish theologian, constituted a major reason for Blake's losing interest in and distancing himself from Swedenborgianism.[11] It was namely the governing belief among Swedenborgian's that Swedenborg's writings were, in fact, the fifth Gospel, presented to him by divine authority in his visions (Rix, 144). Neither would Blake have appreciated Swedenborg's claim to be the only true visionary prophet with unique communication with God and his angels, who singled him out to be the only advocate of the advent of a millennium to be realized in the minds of men. In fact, in many ways Blake believed that Swedenborg's visions were not far-reaching enough. This is obvious on plate 21 of *The Marriage:*

> I have always found that Angels have the vanity to speak of themselves as the only wise; this they do with a confident insolence sprouting from systematic reasoning.

> Thus Swedenborg boasts that what he writes is new; tho' it is only the contents of already publish'd books [21: 1–5, E 42].

And further on the same plate:

> It is so with Swedenborg: he shews the folly of churches & exposes hypocrites, till he imagines that all are religious & himself the single one on earth that ever broke a net.
> Now hear a plain fact: Swedenborg has not written one new truth. Now hear another: he has written all the old falsehoods.
> And now hear the reason. He conversed with Angels who are all religious & conversed not with Devils who all hate religion, for he was incapable thro' conceited notions.
> Thus Swedenborg's writings are a recapitulation of all superficial opinions, and an analysis of the more sublime — but no further [21–2: 8–17, E 42–3].

The terms "religion" and "religious" here have the typically Blakean negative connotation of a state church with priests as representative of its repression of the common man. Hence, there is little doubt that at the time of writing *The Marriage of Heaven and Hell* Blake did not hold Swedenborg in high esteem.

Another point of contention, not only between Blake and Swedenborg, but also in relation to Priestley, was how to read the Bible. With Swedenborg's more matter-of-fact interpretation one may think that Priestley would have had something in common with him on this issue, but this does not appear to have been the case. However, in the main, Swedenborg's rendition stands opposed to Blake's metaphorical reading: "Swedenborg's 'plain and literal' sense of Scripture involved a few passages differently [from Blake] and obscurely interpreted," as Paley points out ("A New Heaven Is Begun," 66). Surely, this must have given Blake some doubts about the compatibility of their respective views on religion.

Most likely Blake had good reason for his skepticism, since Swedenborgianism is definitely the least down-to-earth of the dissenting religions. In our age it is natural to be skeptical to all kinds of visionary experiences. But before discarding Swedenborg's visionary capacity altogether, we might ask ourselves how could Swedenborg, for instance, when visiting Gothenburg on the west coast of Sweden, allegedly describe to people there a fire that was just raging at that very moment in Stockholm on the east coast, 500 kilometers away? And concomitantly, if we renounce

Swedenborg the visionary, how can we then in an acceptable way account for Blake the visionary in the same breath?

Clearly though, to a modern interpreter Swedenborgianism gives rise to a very mixed reception. As much as some of the ideas appear like fabrications of an overheated or intoxicated brain, there are many good points that are worthwhile pondering extra about. Attractive to Blake, for instance, may have been Swedenborg's attempts to reveal the hidden meanings of the Bible through a scrutiny of its internal sense, heavily emphasizing the need for vision. This way Swedenborg wanted to bring back the contemporary corrupt religion to its origins. His critique of church authority could have been another alluring component for Blake. There is also a striking similarity between the grand apocalyptic works of the two prophets, both of them accentuating that the ingredients of everyday human life will be retained in the afterlife, and we will go on to find pleasure in things like food and sex — after death we simply go on with our mundane lives on a higher level. Like Blake, Swedenborg was a pronounced postmillennialist who believed in gradual progress, in contradistinction to the premillennialists who believed in a sudden cataclysmic upheaval of prevailing social structures. Through Swedenborgianism's basic tenets of faith and charity, Swedenborg postulated a millennial renewal of mankind in a brotherhood of man, which was his interpretation of the term charity. This is very close to Blake's philosophy of the forgiveness of sins through Jesus' brotherhood of man in *Jerusalem*. Hence, neither of the two prophets read the Bible literally, as Rix highlights: "Rather, the promise of the New Jerusalem in the Bible was to be interpreted as a mental community of men who would delight in divine virtues. It was a state of peace and brotherhood, to come about as a result of the spiritual conversion within every believer" (105). Swedenborg's interpretation of the Biblical notion that man was created as the image of God is that each individual possesses and employs divine love and charity, an idea reflected in Blake's poem "The Divine Image" from *Songs of Innocence*. Roughly created at the time when Blake participated at the East Cheap conference, this collection of poems is after all one of the clearest manifestations in Blake's writing of his immersion in Swedenborgianism.

However, the areas where Blake seems to have had the most input of Swedenborgian ideas are in their original views and practice of sexuality and their uncommonly great interest in colonial enterprises. Linked to these are important issues like gender relations, marital relations, equality, feminism, slavery and utopian settlements. Interestingly, in these two important issues Swedenborgianism seems to have a lot in common with the Moravians. Moreover, in similarity to the spiritual approach of the Moravian Church it was Swedenborg's aim that the New Jerusalem Church was to be a church of the spirit. A further parallel was that Swedenborgianism was also allowed within the ranks of the Church of England at that time. So, there is good reason to believe that Blake found many positive and inspiring components in these two Churches. If we only had more substantial evidence, we might even have claimed that Blake's very personal religious belief was chiefly made up by components from Moravianism and Swedenborgianism.

In his otherwise competent discussion of Swedenborgianism and its links to Blake, Robert Rix seems nonplussed by a tricky passage from *Milton*. Rix rightly states that Blake differed with Swedenborg over doctrines of justification, but he fails to see the Moravian influence on the two passages from *Milton* that he examines. Both are most definitely references to the Moravians' celebration of the crucifixion of Christ with their uncommonly strong veneration for his wounds and blood. As much as Blake criticizes Swedenborg for the fact that his writings "deny the value of the Saviour's blood" (22: 54, E 118), this instance is also a strong affirmation of his immersion in Moravianism. This is similarly the case in the earlier passage discussed by Rix: "Christ took on Sin in the Virgins Womb, & put it off on the Cross" (5: 3, E 98). Significantly, later on the same plate as the previous passage, there is another reference to "the death of the Cross" (22: 58, E 118). As we shall see later, there are similar instances in *Jerusalem*.

So, although it is sometimes difficult to understand what drew Blake, with his strong antinomian inclination, to the increasingly conservative Swedenborgianism, the interest and fascination is undeniably there. If we go to the very bottom of it and penetrate the affinities between Blake and Swedenborg, what eventually stands out are the two issues of utopian colonialism and sexual politics. As we shall see, the two are most of the time intriguingly intertwined and mutually interdependent in the treatment of the Swedenborgians. It is my overriding argument that as much as these ideas attracted Blake in the first place, they also served to alienate him from the New Jerusalem Church after the ultimate downfall and collapse of their too idealistic project.[12]

The colonial, mostly utopian, enterprises of the Swedenborgians were mainly the fruit of extraordinary individual interests and efforts. The incentive for this was probably twofold: the general search for knowledge during the Enlightenment era made possible by the burgeoning industrialization, and the Swedenborgian belief that there existed a divine connection to Africa.

The focus on the African continent can be traced back to Swedenborg's belief that Africans have retained the clearest intuition of God. There was also the general notion that the lost books of the Bible, the Apocrypha, were hidden somewhere in Africa. Of particular interest to the Swedenborgians was the *Book of Enoch*, which had been rediscovered in Ethiopia in an Ethiopic version a century earlier, and the first English translation of which appeared in 1821 (Paley, *Traveller*, 266). This finding was greatly contested, however, and many scholars believed at least parts of it to be forgeries. Greater certainty was gained when the Scottish traveler James Bruce brought three copies back to Europe in 1773. In spite of this, according to leading Swedenborgians there still were other lost Bible books to be found.

The rediscovery of the *Book of Enoch* was something that greatly engaged Blake, as Paley explains: "It is not surprising that such a combination of the supernatural-erotic and the apocalyptic stimulated the imaginations of poets such as Lord Byron and Thomas Moore and artists such as John Flaxman and William Blake" (*Traveller*, 268). *Enoch* provided Blake with rich material that fitted well with his radical penchant: "William Blake's drawings for the *Book of Enoch* present scenes of sexual ferocity and visionary power" (Paley, *Traveller*, 269).

It was the urge to find the lost Bible books that led a number of explorers with Swedenborgian sympathies to undertake some of the first expeditions to the west coast of Africa, with the intention of continuing to the heart of the continent where they presumed the books were located. One of these was the Swedish philanthropist Carl-Bernard Wadström, who was to be one of the founders and one of the main organizers of the New Jerusalem Church in 1789 and whom William and Catherine Blake met at that convention. But already in 1787 he had been on a voyage to Sierra Leone. More importantly, on the 1788 expedition Wadström rescued the African teenage slave Peter Panah and brought him to London. Panah was portrayed together with his benefactor Wadström instructing him from the works of Swedenborg by the famous Swedish portraitist Carl Fredrik von Breda. Recently David Worrall has intriguingly suggested that

Panah is "The Little Black Boy" of Blake's *Songs of Innocence* ("Thel in Africa," conference paper 6).

The other Swedish former and main organizer of the New Jerusalem Church, August Nordenskjöld, had also been to Africa before that meeting and was to return there in 1792 only to die after setting out in search of the natives with closer connection to God, and possibly also to look for the remaining lost books of the Bible.[13] In spite of the warnings from Wadström and others, Nordenskjöld set off during the rainy season to look for native tribes but did not get very far and instead of reaching the heart of Africa died of rheumatism in Sierra Leone. Wadström said of his friend's attempt: "He signified an ardent desire to penetrate immediately into the country, where he always hoped to find an innocent, hospitable people, among whom he could pursue his researches" (Worrall, "Thel in Africa," conference paper 20, original source not indicated).

Nordenskjöld, of course, was another of the ninety-five original formers of the Swedenborgian society that Blake met at Great East Cheap. Together with his brother Carl-Fredric he had formed a Swedish Swedenborg association at Norrköping, close to where the Swedenborgian library is now located,[14] before his African expeditions and coming to England. Notably, the two Nordenskjölds and Wadström were well connected to high Swedish authorities, who appointed all of them to major offices in the mining industry. We know that Swedenborg himself for several years occupied the top position within that trade as overseer of mines.

It appears that the Swedish influence on early Swedenborgianism was substantial, which is only natural bearing in mind the Swedish origin of Emanuel Swedenborg. However, the works of Swedenborg were soon banned in Sweden. He had to look elsewhere to find a printer of his works, and was able to do so in Amsterdam and London, which was a major reason that he ended up in England. That Swedenborg was practically exiled from Sweden is remarkable for several reasons. First, he wrote in Latin, something that must have made an obscure writer even more obscure. Sweden at that time was, like most of Western Europe, heavily influenced by France, and the French language was the language of the court and the upper classes. Latin was by then out of fashion, and only some clergymen and a few learned people were in good command of it. The expulsion of Swedenborg becomes even more remarkable as we know that Sweden at that time was enjoying a high-point of culture and education in the wake of the European wave of Enlightenment and the generous support and interest of the Swedish monarch Gustav III. As this was one of the absolute heydays of learning and research in Swedish history, one might certainly wonder why the great achievements of Swedenborg were not appreciated to a larger extent by his own contemporaries. This is particularly strange since at the time of leaving the country Swedenborg had yet not started to write his theological tracts, and his publications consisted of rather important findings in the natural sciences.

But it seems that the perception of the Swedenborgians in Sweden was quite dubious during the second half of the eighteenth century. Remarkably, and intriguingly, some well-known Swedenborgians were accused of being accomplices in the assassination of King Gustav III during a masque at the Royal Opera in Stockholm in 1792.

Undeniably, the basic tenet of Swedenborgianism is conjugial love. In the Swedenborgian context this is an all-embracing concept. As much as it provided their colonial enterprises, and, particularly, Wadström and Nordenskjöld's 1789 Sierra Leone project, with the basic social and political principle, it was also the foundation of their sexual politics. In fact, the utopian society of Sierra Leone was to have conjugial love as its basic principle. A key passage from Wadström's *Plan for a Free Community* appropriately sums these ideas up:

> The Conjugal [sic] Alliance of the Community, which is between the Sexes, or between the Understanding in the Man and the Will in the Woman; or, Man's Wisdom and Woman's Love, because upon this depends intirely [sic] the improvement of the very elements in all Communities, which are Marriages, or the Conjugal Unions, and not, either Man or Woman separately considered [29–30].

As Wadström further claims, "Every Marriage is representative, in miniature, of the Civil society in it's principles or beginnings" (v).

Much in line with Blake's notion of gender equality with the union of male and female, the partnership of man and woman lies at the core of this fundamental doctrine. And as in Blake, the basic desire is for man and woman to become joined into one. This is quite obvious in Swedenborg's most basic definition of "conjugial love": "Love taken by itself is nothing but a desire and hence an impulse to be joined; conjugial love is an impulse to be joined into one" (II 37: 1, 40). Swedenborg also gives a clear distinction between the highest form of love, "conjugial love," and sexual love in general: "Sexual love is love directed to and shared with several persons of the other sex, but conjugial love is directed to and shared with one person of the other sex" (II 48: 1, 52). Here, and elsewhere, we come across a strikingly premature notion of equality where there is no distinguishing and degrading hierarchy between the sexes; instead, Swedenborg innovatively talks about "person[s] of the other sex." It is therefore easy when first glancing at these propositions to read in quite a radical notion of equality to Swedenborgianism. However, it is not as far-reaching as one might first think. Considering the then still strong patriarchal dominance of society, the Swedenborgians of course proposed, if not a radical, at least a remarkably egalitarian alternative society. It is not a wholly unfounded comment that Swedenborg was at least partly an early advocate of feminism. But from a modern perspective both the works of Swedenborg and the Sierra Leone plan contain a number of male conservative lynch-pins, which lends something of a sour aftertaste to an ostensibly egalitarian credo.

Perhaps most striking is the Swedenborgian idea of concubinage. Like the other Swedenborgian tenets on love and sexuality the work where this is most elaborately described is *Conjugial Love*. Although taking a concubine in general should not be allowed, Swedenborg claims that in certain circumstances it is acceptable: "Having a concubine without association with a wife is not unlawful, when it is for lawful, just and truly weighty reasons" (xx 467: 1, 436). These weighty reasons might be sickness and disabilities of various kinds, but more remarkably also lack of sexual interest from one of the parties. Here this exclusively refers to the woman, so we have another flagrant example of a conservative component in an overall radical belief. The works of Swedenborg are simply written from a very male perspective, whether we consider them patriarchal or not.

Concubinage was also one of the predominant ideas behind the aborted Sierra Leone project, and we find it expressed in several passages of Wadström's *Plan for a Free Community*. For instance he writes that "[b]y Anti-Conjugial Life, I do not here mean the attachment of one unmarried Man to one free Woman, and simply Concubinage, which under certain regulations never ought to be forbidden in a Free State" (31). Just like in *Conjugial Love*, we find certain concessions for the male sex only: "This Love of the Sex in every Male has two kinds of Eruption, or two channels of Ebullition; the one extends more and more towards various objects, and the other concentrates all its force into one, and never strays beyond its proper circle" (35). What seems to have been a natural mode of thinking to the Swedenborgians was later to be questioned by both Blake and Coleridge. Coleridge definitely lost interest in Pantisocrasy when Southey insisted that the women should be sexually shared among the men of the community, and their joint utopian project was abandoned for good. Perhaps this was also a contributing reason that the Sierra Leone colony was never realized.

Whether Blake, as many commentators believe, distanced himself from Swedenborgianism from 1790 onwards or not, there are arguably several notions that stayed with him throughout his artistic career. Notably, some of them are central values shared between the Swedenborgians and the Moravians. As much as this shows the affinity between these two denominations, it also gives us a good idea of the difficulty to appoint either of these two religious orientations, or any other, directly and exclusively to Blake. Blake never adhered to any particular creed or way of thinking but his own.

That there are obvious similarities between Moravians and Swedenborgians is not that surprising as we know that Emanuel Swedenborg was a regular visitor to the Fetter Lane society after he arrived in London in 1744. In spite of this, it appears that Swedenborg was somewhat skeptical towards the Moravians, something that Hessayon a little surprisingly notes: "Swedenborg showed an aversion to the Quakers and expressed an equally low opinion of the Moravians, whose services at their chapel in Fetter Lane he had attended in 1744." He was also censorious towards Count Zinzendorf, whom he claimed to have met several times in the spiritual world (25). Remarkably, until very recently no record has been found in the Moravian archives about Swedenborg's participation in their activities. But we have helpful documentation in a note by Swedenborg's landlord John Paul Brockmer that "the Baron [...] went every Sunday to the chapel of the Moravians in Fetter Lane" (Schuchard, *Mrs Blake*, 60). It is precisely the knowledge about his landlord Paul Brockmer that has now provided us with the only reference to Swedenborg of the Moravians, from 1745, freshly discovered in the archives by Keri Davies: "The Swedishman at B^r Brokmer's [sic], that was lately besides himself is now better again, and goes out" (*Moravian Church Library and Archive* AB38 Minutes of Saturday Conferences, 1744–5). It is without doubt that this refers to Swedenborg's fit of near madness on the doorstep of his landlord's house in spring 1745 (Schuchard, *Mrs Blake*, 60).

There are two intriguing points with the timing here. First, Swedenborg's affiliation with the Moravians coincides with their most radical period, Sifting Time 1743–53, when experimentation of sexual practices was at its pinnacle. Secondly, this also coincided with the period when Blake's mother Catherine and her first husband Thomas Armitage and Blake's possible uncle John had their most active years in the church. Particularly, Catherine seems to have been a devoted Moravian member at the time.

If we are to believe Schuchard, Swedenborg had a very active sex life and was highly aware of new, experimental sexual techniques (*Mrs Blake*, 77–83). As always, the focus lay on the regular exercise of marital intercourse, what the Moravians called the mystical marriage and Swedenborg would later refer to as conjugial love, and a veneration of the male and female genitals. Often Swedenborg's descriptions of the genitals took the form of detailed anatomical accounts of the various parts. Much of this was recorded in his treatise *The Generative Organs,* which was published posthumously. The descriptions here and in other places were quite explicit and to the point: "She with her hand touched my member, and it grew large, larger than it ever had been. I turned round and applied myself; it bent, yet it went in. She said it was long" (*Journal of Dreams* no. 171, quoted in *Mrs Blake*, 81). The ultimate goal for both Moravians and Swedenborgians, as well as for Blake, was the reunion of male and female:

> The parts of the woman answer to those of the male, as though they had first been naturally united, and afterwards separated; and when united they resembled only a single body.... The female parts so correspond to the male, that during the time of carnal copulation they resemble one and not two bodies, and so far coalesce that in the moment of orgasm [Swedenborg, *Generative Organs*, 155–60, quoted in *Mrs Blake*, 97].[15]

It adds to this issue that Swedenborg in *Conjugial Love* visualized the resting-position of the male and female in afterlife with the bodies being united as in coitus (Rix, 100).

One thing that Swedenborgianism had in common with the Moravians was the emphasis of the importance of the constant exercise of the conjugial rights, in other words, sexual intercourse. In his *Plan* Wadström writes: "Nothing however is more true, than that the Love of the Sex, and the constant exercise thereof, which is the Virile Potency, is the very basis to the affection of all other kinds of permanent Powers" (35). Indeed, it was inscribed that in the Sierra Leone colony sexual intercourse was to be incorporated into the very notion of citizenship: "The true exercise of civil duties is founded in an unboundedly active Industry, in what is useful; and true Religion, in an unlimited exercise of regular Conjugal Life" (xi). A similar idea was prominent among the Moravians, as we shall shortly see.

Another similarity between the two congregations was an unusual fixation of the genital organs, male as well as female. They both professed that the original impulse of the exercise of Conjugal Life naturally springs from the genital region. In *Conjugial Love* Swedenborg writes: "On account of the remarkable connexion that exists between the chest cavity and the genital region, the delights of one become in the other the delights of conjugial love" (VIII 188: 8, 188). In this way true spirituality gives rise to conjugial love, he maintains: "Here everything which derives from the prime source is present at once, and together with their successive stages brings about conjugial love" (VIII 183: 2, 186). As we know, Blake, in *The Marriage* and elsewhere, stresses the interdependence of body and soul, and in *Jerusalem* it is the spiritual harmony that initiates the reunion of man and woman in conjugial love. Furthermore, in his designs Blake shows great awareness of the function of the body, with his portrayal of mostly nude figures.

Moravianism

Moravianism is the least well-known of the three dissenting religions discussed here, and probably the most obscure. Although the new discoveries have been an eye-opener to many Blakeans and to others with similar interests, and thus have improved our knowledge about the Moravians, much of their background probably remains largely unknown and it will surely take some time before that church gains the obvious status in Blake studies that Swedenborgianism enjoys. Because of its rather ancient beginnings and geographic spread, the history of the Moravians is not easily told. Another complication is the congregation's quite unusual relation to the state church in different countries, not least in England. One piece of evidence of this is that Blake's parents chose to christen their child William in the Anglican Church at St. James, Piccadilly. This goes to show that, if Catherine was still adhering to her previous Moravian beliefs, she only followed their practice to remain within one's national church even while participating in the affairs of the Brethren (Podmore, *The Moravian Church in England*, 1728-1760, 176–77). Although it was first established in Europe in the fifteenth century and, barring a few not so prosperous periods, has been an active religious force since then, Moravianism has never attracted a large number of followers. But, the few enthusiasts of the sect have always been very dedicated, and, like the Unitarians and the Swedenborgians, for a decisive period of their history they had a leader with a very strong personality.

In the case of the Moravians the leader was a German count by the name Nicholas Louis von Zinzendorf, a much talented character who more or less defines the most active period of the Moravians during the eighteenth century. Born in 1700 into a noble family at Dresden, Saxony, he early showed an uncommonly great aptitude for reclusive activities like philosophizing and studying — particularly the Bible and other religious tracts. "I can say with truth that my heart was religiously inclined as far back as I can recollect," Zinzendorf himself explains *(Büdingische Sammlungen*, Hagen, *Old Landmarks*, 120, in Weinlick, 19). To be noble and pious is an unusual combination, as Weinlick maintains: "The union of piety and nobility is one of the keys to an appreciation of Zinzendorf" (21). For better or for worse he was a count, and in his illustrious career there was more than one occasion when he made good use of his noble background.

It was particularly useful in connection to the foremost Moravian task, missionary calling. The establishment of the Moravian church in England and the British North American colonies among other places formed the life of Count Zinzendorf over the following decades. After finally being ordained as a pastor in 1734, the Count dedicated the rest of his life to spreading the Word and founding new Moravian congregations throughout the world as a constant vagrant with no stationary home. The fact that he was banished from Saxony due to growing opposition and disagreement within the Moravian ranks in 1736 made his decision easier. That year the Pilgrim-congregation was formed and the most active period of the Moravian missions was thus begun. "With the banishment of the Count from Saxony, a new period in the history of the Renewed Church commenced," as it reads in the *History of the Unitas Fratrum* (Moravian Brethren, 70). Zinzendorf himself told another of the leaders, David Nitschman, neatly summing up the Moravian missionary and nomadic venture:

> Even without this prohibition I could not have gone to Herrnhut within the next ten years, to remain for any length of time, for we have now to form a Pilgrim-Church, and to make known the Saviour to the world. Henceforward, that place will be our home, where there is most to be done for Christ [Moravian Brethren, 69].

One of the first countries Zinzendorf visited was England, in 1737. By that time the English Moravian Church had already been formed by previous missionaries, but the Zinzendorfian impact was imperative in definitely establishing the first English congregation at Fetter Lane in 1742. "A stay of nearly two months in London laid the foundation for the permanent establishment of the Moravians in the English-speaking world," as Weinlick tells us (135). He also made sure that the Moravians remained un-severed from the English Protestant church, a fact that proved to be of great importance, not least in William Blake's peculiar religious context.

However, true to his nomadic way of living, Zinzendorf was not to stay long in London. He followed another of the great Moravians, Spangenberg, to help him establish the community in America. The *History* again: "Spangenberg commenced the work in North America. In the autumn of 1735, he went to Georgia, accompanied by ten colonists. As, however, great hindrances presented themselves, he proceeded to Pennsylvania" (Moravian Brethren, 84–5). The Moravians had earlier set America as one of their main missionary targets, and in 1741 Zinzendorf went there to visit their Pennsylvanian colony. "[T]he Moravians indelibly took on the nature of an interchurch society," Weinlick claims (185), and that was one of the main purposes of Zinzendorf's American spell — to organize an effective union of different churches. Working hard over a couple of years to unite the various newly established religious congregations, he was never as successful in the new world as in the old and therefore returned to Europe in 1743. Zinzendorf eventually settled again at Herrnhut in 1755, where he lived his final years and died in 1760.[16]

Zinzendorf's massive influence on the Moravian Church is underscored in the following extract from Weinlick's important biography:

> It has taken five years, from 1722 to 1727, for the Brotherhood, later to be known as the Renewed Moravian Church, to come into being. The next five years saw the emergence of most of the features which determined the peculiar role of the Brethren in the church world of Europe and America for the next two centuries. At the very cen-

ter of this development was Zinzendorf himself. The year 1727 marks the time when Zinzendorfian Pietism began to diverge from its parent stock. In the years immediately following, Herrnhut became the kind of village which was to serve as a model for the twenty or more Moravian "settlement" congregations founded during the next fifty years. These communities were a blend of Pietism, the discipline of the Bohemian and Moravian Brethren, and the genius of an individual [83].

Briefly sketched, Moravianism is a relatively ancient church dating back to the fifteenth century. It had its origins as the Church of the Bohemian Brethren, or Unitas Fratrum, in continental Europe in the Moravian and Bohemian regions, in what is now the Czech Republic. More precisely, it was founded in 1457 by a group of Hussites, followers of the teachings of the Czech reformer John Hus (c. 1369–1415).[17] This was a pre–Lutheran reform movement, which reacted against church corruption in these regions around that time. The Moravian church has never been a large congregation and has experienced turbulence and several swings in popularity as well as geographical location over the years. Its first peak came in the early days of the fifteenth century, but it was then more or less eradicated in the Thirty Years War, only to rise fully again in 1722 in Saxony on Count Zinzendorf's estate at Herrnhut. It was then that its indisputable high point under the leadership of the charismatic Zinzendorf occurred and some missionaries traveled to London with the intention to continue further west to the British colonies in the present-day United States. In London, however, they intermingled with an already existing religious group at Fetter Lane and thus developed a permanent Moravian Congregation from the initiative of August Gottlieb Spangenberg and Peter Böhler. Although Moravianism has never had a big following, its disciples have always been devoted and remain so to this day with settlements throughout the world. The east coast of the United States is a particular stronghold, which has become its present day headquarters.[18]

As indicated above, the Moravian Church in England was formed by a small number of missionaries from Herrnhut in Saxony, who first arrived in 1722. This leads us to the third major Moravian figure of this period, Peter Böhler: "Spangenberg in the years 1734 and 1735, and the Count, on occasion of his visit in 1735, had taken preliminary action in England, though without permanent results. The real founder, however, of the work of the Brethren in this country, was Peter Böhler" (Moravian Brethren,

83). The group soon acquired a small but dedicated following in London, and in 1738 the Fetter Lane Society was established, which saw the Wesley brothers John and Charles as early members, and came to heavily influence the ideas of John Wesley. The Moravians had already spread northwards in England, with Yorkshire as an early major congregation and, significantly, an affiliation in Nottingham. The *History* gives us an account of the events:

> In April, 1741, the Society for the furtherance of the Gospel was founded under his [Spangenberg's] auspices, and on the 10th of November, 1742, a Society in connection with the Church of the Brethren was settled in London. In the same year, Spangenberg, accompanied by Töltschig and Böhler, proceeded into Yorkshire. In that county a great awakening had taken place among the working classes, under the preaching of Mr. Ingham, a clergyman of the Church of England, and the Brethren were earnestly requested to take the spiritual charge of those who were under conviction [Moravian Brethren, 92].

Eventually, the Fetter Lane Chapel was registered under the Toleration Act on 7 September 1742, when the Brethren authorized James Hutton to take out a license for the Fetter Lane Society on the terms granted to dissenters at that time.[19] It was a striking paradox that the Moravians were then forced to register their churches as "Dissenting meeting-houses," even though eighteenth-century Moravians no more regarded themselves as dissenters than did eighteenth-century Methodists. While Count Zinzendorf still stood firm in keeping the Moravians as a society only, an evangelical group working alongside or even within the Church of England, he also looked upon registration as a step in the direction of denominationalism.[20]

Fetter Lane quickly became a popular meeting-point, not only for Moravians but also for other people with an alternative religious outlook. For instance, we know that for some time Emanuel Swedenborg was a regular visitor. The Fetter Lane Congregation provided a permanent base in London to take advantage of the evangelistic opportunities in England opened up by the contemporary evangelical revival and to facilitate missionary activities in the American colonies.[21] The passing on 24 June 1749 of "An Act for Encouraging the People Known by the Name of the Unitas Fratrum, or United Brethren, to settle in His Majesties Colonies in America" gave the Fetter Lane Congregation a new standing in the eyes of Londoners.²² The act significantly functioned as a preamble that acknowledged the United Brethren as an "ancient Protestant Episcopal Church."²³ Hereafter, the Moravian Church was in official alliance with the Church of England with status as an Episcopal church. The Moravians saw themselves in no sense as dissenters, but, on the contrary, as a sister church of the Church of England.²⁴ "The Moravians henceforth [1749] had status in Britain and her dependencies," Weinlick informs us (197). Hence, the Moravians had a special standing vis-à-vis the old Church of England. "The position of this body in England during the eighteenth century was quite unusual [...] they were and then again were not Dissenters," Davies writes, indicating the unsevered ties between the Moravians and the Church of England (*William Blake in Contexts*, 284–85). Thus the Moravians became the leaders of the great Evangelical Revival, as E. R. Hassé has confirmed: "It not only stirred England to its very depths, but it shaped the course of our people at a most critical period" (XI). Appearing in England at a crucial time in the mid–eighteenth century at the height of Enlightenment ideals and just before the revolutionary commotion of the final decades, the Moravian Church usurped a unique position in English religious life, something which made dissenting congregations suspicious and envious. "Indeed," states Keri Davies, "the dissenting churches viewed the Moravian Brethren with hostility" (Davies, "The Winepress of Love," 5).

The Moravians may not ever have had great numbers of followers, but their importance is emphatically shown by the fact that they indirectly influenced and gave an impetus to the beginnings of Methodism, which was the dominant church of dissent during Blake's time. The influence becomes more palpable as the first leading Methodists, the Wesley brothers John and Charles, were among the original founders of the Moravians before they broke away to form their new congregation. With the help of the Moravian influence John Wesley's Methodist mission significantly changed the eighteenth-century British religious landscape through the awakening of the so-called religion of the heart.

There were many features of the Moravian Church that certainly must have been intriguing to Blake. For one thing, Moravianism is not at all doctrinaire but indeed very spiritual. In spite of being loosely tied to the Church of England, they were far from a state-dependent Church dominated by priesthood and rules, a notion omnipresent in Blake's work. Jesus was the crucial figure and, like Blake, they emphasized a humanitarian and Christian brotherhood of man.

In contrast to the Unitarians, feeling and passion, not reason, were believed to be the foundation of the faculties. Most extremely, and importantly to Blake, Zinzendorf rejected reason as the primary force of the imagination; instead he emphasized eroticism. This is of course also close to the ideas of Emanuel Swedenborg. In line with this, they intriguingly professed the glory of sexuality, a significant role for the female, and to some extent even equality between the sexes. The most extreme expression of these was their strong accentuation of a common veneration of the genitals, the male as well as the female. They cherished the belief that since Jesus was born with a penis, this organ should be the beauty of the male body and not mentioned with shame; and since he was born through the female organ the same should go for that. "In his passionate sermons and hymns," Schuchard writes, "Zinzendorf praised the human genitals—penis and vagina—as emblems of the 'humanation' of Jesus, who took on the full range of human nature and thus sanctified not only the spirit but the body of men and women" ("The 'Secret' and the 'Gift'" 211). Blake of course includes a great number of nude figures in his art and illustrations, even though the genitals are not always that blatantly demarcated. On the other hand, there are some examples of the other extreme, with enlarged and clearly emphasized genitals. Perhaps the best evidence of this are the intriguing sketches in the manuscript of *The Four Zoas*.

The male-female union in the form of marriage was another cornerstone in the Moravian creed and, remarkably, "married people [...] were not looked upon as lawfully married, unless they performed the conjugal Duties in the Presence of the Elders" (Rimius, *Candid Narrative*, 119). Not only does this remind us of Blake's early ideas of "free" love, a Wollstonecraftian notion paraphrased mainly in *Visions of the Daughters of Albion*, but also the Swedenborgian tenet of "conjugial love," for instance expressed in Wadström's *Plan for a Free Community* where the urgency of everyday exercise of the Love of the Sex was emphasized *(Plan,* xxx). It seems, though, that the Moravian attitude regarding this issue was more extreme and they greatly emphasized the union of the soul with Christ through sexual intercourse, what they called the Mystical Marriage. In this way they attempted to overcome sexual desire by making sex sacred. Weinlick elaborates on this notion:

> The expression of love for Christ took on strong sexual connotations. There was an undue exaltation of marriage as the symbol of the marriage between Christ and the soul of the believer, and in this

exaltation sexual terminology was freely employed. Earthly marriages were looked upon as proxies in anticipation of the final union of Christ and the believer. The marriage relationship was idealized in long discourses and hymns [200].

In general, the Moravians found the missionary cause to be the most important to their doctrine. With their many overseas colonial enterprises and their attempt to establish a utopian colony in Herrnhut, the Moravians show a similar inclination as the Swedenborgians with their Sierra Leone project, which was discussed by Blake and the other delegates at the 1789 East Cheap conference. Indeed, it was through the missionary zeal of the second wave Bohemians that Moravianism by the mid–eighteenth century became established in England, and somewhat later in the United States. Coming at a very critical and fluctuating period of English history just before the French Revolution, the great Evangelical Revival in 1738 shaped the course of the people. "[F]ew events in our national history have surpassed it in importance," as Hassé puts it (XI). Ever since then the Moravians have been permanently present in English religious and social life.

If the religious mission was the primary concern for the Moravians, education was nearly as important and a natural major ingredient in the missionary projects. As Hassé informs us, "The Moravian teaching was in essence to be found in the Thirty-Nine Articles, and was entirely based upon the New Testament" (39), which again emphasizes their strong fixation on Jesus. Already in the days of their first community in Bohemia in the sixteenth century learning was vital to them. Bohemians managed to become the most well-educated people in Europe much thanks to the outstanding Moravian printing presses (Hassé, X). When they settled in England they carried on their successful work with education. This seems to be a trait they share with the Unitarians, and like them they created schools with a particular atmosphere and a sometimes original curriculum.

One important outcome of the Moravians' advanced ideas on learning and education, and presumably their convenient access to printing presses, was that they published the first Protestant hymn-book (Hassé, X). There are several accounts of their fondness of singing hymns: "A great Part of their Worship consists in singing. They preferd [sic] that Children in particular, are instructed in their Religion by hymns" (Rimius, *Candid Narrative*, 10). Interestingly, John Wesley, who was closely linked to the Moravians for a period, translated some of their hymns into English (Podmore, *The Moravian Church in England*, 32). The particular hymnody of the Moravians may well have influenced and inspired Blake when he was creating the *Songs*.

As for the religious teaching and message of the Moravians, it was very much centered on Christ. Their focus on Christ, his brotherhood and mutual love, is not far from Blake's mature ideas. As Hassé develops: "The doctrine was largely based upon Luther's teaching, but it differed from Lutheranism in this, that it made the person of Christ, and fellowship with Him, its central point, rather than any formulated confession of faith" (41–2). We come even closer to Blake and his indisputable detestation of state religion when we understand that the Moravians believed that every single human being had the freedom to interpret the Word of God, and that there should be no reliance on any kind of priesthood.

A further similarity to Blake was their insistence upon the need for all Christians to unite. "Another important feature of Moravianism was living in community," Podmore explains (*The Moravian Church in England*, 52). But just like Blake, they were different from the other dissenting groups by stressing mutual love and devotion to Christ. This is what we find expressed in Blake's three great epics, especially *Jerusalem*, in the concepts of forgiveness of sins and the Brotherhood of Jesus. The following passage from Hassé serves well to illustrate the proximity of Blake and the Moravians on this issue:

> Christ had become to them something more than a great historic figure of the past, far more than "the highest authority," more even than the saviour of the world. He was to them "a living, bright reality," the one all-dominating factor of their lives, their own personal Saviour, their Friend and Brother, as well as their Master [43–4].

The Moravians' fanatic worship of Christ had its most extreme expression, linked to their erotic emphasis, in their unique and eccentric focus on the wounds and blood of Christ's body—particularly the side-wounds. It is because of this that the Moravians have gained the reputation as "the visible wound-church." According to the *History of the Moravian Brethren*, the background for the focus can be found in "the atonement made for sin by the blood of Jesus, and happiness in communion with Him" (Moravian Brethren, 85). Most bizarre to modern eyes may seem the correspondence they drew between Christ's side-wound and the female genitals. The exaltation of the side-wound as a symbol of the vagina during their most intense and radical period, the Sifting Time in the mid–eighteenth century, took unhealthy and almost ridiculous proportions. According to several sources, even lascivious sexual perversions such as orgies of group sex frequently occurred. Marsha Keith Schuchard mentions that during this period the Moravians at Herrnhut had named a room the "blue chamber," where couples had something called "liturgical sex" in what they thought of as a "bordello" (*Why Mrs. Blake Cried*, 53). It is said that Zinzendorf's son, the flamboyant and charismatic Christian Renato, who had just arrived to London from Herrnhut, was a key player in the sexual rites and therefore ran the risk of being expelled. By using his great charm, however, he somehow managed to stay in the Fetter Lane congregation. The Moravian Church was never again to act as amorally and sexually lax as it had during the Sifting years.[25]

The adventurous and provocative period under Zinzendorf with its attempts in sexual, spiritual and racial liberation was both the most creative and the most controversial time in the history of the Moravians. The Sifting Time led to an uproar among the more conservative members of the church and the period became buried in their archives, never to be brought into the open for centuries. This called for a severe backlash and a moral purge of the whole church, and several people were literally thrown out. According to Moravian historians, this was a period of excess, often sexual, which was centered around the obsessed fascination with the wounds and blood of Christ:

> The Sifting Period was a distortion of a basically sound emphasis upon the atoning death of Christ. Its outward manifestation was a morbid concentration and wordplay upon the blood and wounds of the crucified Christ and a simulated irresponsibility of behaviour supposed to be a demonstration of childlike faith [Weinlick, 198].

It appears that Blake knew about this period and the emphasis on the wounds and blood of Christ and was somehow fascinated by it. We find this idea expressed in the extraordinary poem "The Grey Monk" from *The Pickering Manuscript*:

> The blood red ran from the Grey Monks side
> His hands & feet were wounded wide
> His Body bent his arms & knees
> Like to the roots of ancient trees
> His eye was dry no tear could flow
> A hollow groan first spoke his woe
> He trembled & shudderd upon the Bed [E 489]

It is all the more remarkable bearing in mind that the Pickering poems were written rather late, probably at the beginning of the nineteenth century. This piece of evidence certainly demonstrates the profound legacy and influence of basic Moravian beliefs in Blake's upbringing. It also refutes the view of Robert Rix that "the distinctive Passion-centered symbolism of sucking the wounds of the crucified Jesus, by which Moravianism was recognized, does not register in his vocabulary or imagery" (9). A bit further on Rix somewhat oddly singles out *Poetical Sketches* as the prominent example of Moravian influence in Blake's work, and even conducts a brief analysis of some of the poems in this early volume, privately published through the helpful assistance of some of Blake's friends. I will give further evidence of Blake's Moravianism in my discussion of "The Grey Monk" in the chapter "Blake's Sexuality."

On the other hand, Rix gives a valuable account of the importance of music and painting to the Moravians. They had a long-standing tradition of communal hymn-singing, which may well have influenced Blake at an early age. This would rhyme well with our knowledge that Blake sang his *Songs* backed with music. We have an account of him performing his songs in this way at the literary salons of Reverend and Mrs. Mathew in the 1780s. Also, painting was important to the Moravians, and according to Rix several paintings were displayed during their love-feasts. To enhance the spirituality of the paintings these were often displayed without frames (Rix, 10).

The goal of the Moravians was a millennium of brotherhood of peace, after Christianity had been restored to its foundational roots. This is of course emphatically reflected in Blake's prophetic writing, particularly in the three major epics. Much like the Moravians, Blake tried to reunite different religious expressions, something which is obvious for instance in the directions of the three prose sections of *Jerusalem:* "To the Jews," "To the Deists," and "To the Christians," respectively. Through this preliminary step man and woman will be reunited in the apocalypse, and accordingly all men will be one. For one thing, "this will come to pass by an improvement of sensual enjoyment," as Blake writes in Plate 14 of *The Marriage of Heaven and Hell* (E 39).

Interestingly, there are a number of features in the Moravian doctrine that allow us, to a greater extent than the Swedenborgians, to call them proto-feminists, with a naturally inherent striving for gender equality. For instance, Rimius tells us that "[a]t all Hours, whether Day or Night, some Persons, of both Sexes, are appointed by Rotation to pray for the Society" (10). Hence, besides the Single Brethren there were also the Single Sisters and among their many festivities and love-feasts there was a particular celebration they called the Mutterfest. Significantly, Zinzendorf wanted both male and female to equally share the image of God and therefore made the feminine one part of the Trinity and visualized an androgynous Christ-figure. It is further known that they worshipped not only the male Jesus, but also the female in calling him their Mama Jesua or their Mother, thus also giving him the feminine gender (Rimius, 43). And as we have already seen, in their remarkable fixation on the genitals, both the male and the female organs were equally strongly venerated.

Furthermore, the Moravians went a long way to accommodate their female worshippers as well as the male ones. With the erotic union of believers with Christ in a metaphorical sense as a foundation, they came upon the original solution to make all souls female. This unique idea is evident in their hymnology and poetry. The following hymn makes clear that we are all brides of Christ, men as well as women:

> Know'st thou, that the Saviour
> Shew'd thee grace and favour
> When a Criminal?
> 'Twas his Blood did ransom
> Thy soul from the dungeon
> But as Yesterday;
> And To-Day, to thy great joy,
> Thou art next unto him placed,
> As his Bride caressed
> [United Brethren of Christ, *A Collection of Hymns of the Children of God in all Ages, from the Beginning till Now*, 74].

While souls are female, Jesus is the universal husband. Ultimately, both men and women will be married to Christ as he is the only true male. Keri Davies believes that this could well have stirred Blake's imagination and intriguingly argues along these lines:

> This view of the soul's relationship to Christ has interesting implications for Zinzendorf's anthropology. It appears that Zinzendorf was seeking a theory of androgyny, at least for men. He does say that in the future there will be only one gender, the female.[26] Perhaps a Moravian spirituality lies behind Blake's ideas concerning

the sexual union of man and woman as a means to restore the originally androgynous state of the human being in the fallen world[27] ["Blake and the Moravians," 11].

If we accept Davies's claim here, it would imply that there is a Moravian basis to Blake's whole mythological system in the prophetic poems.

The years when Blake formed his unique philosophy by creating a complex mythological system very much his own, the late 1780s and early 1790s, was a crucial time in British history when radical views, formerly unexpressed, suddenly emerged. A profound optimism flourished all over Britain, inspired by the two revolutions in America and France. Artists, poets, artisans, petty merchants and other minority groups organized themselves in various radical societies throughout the country, and particularly so in Blake's native London.[28]

Religious life was also influenced by the new ways of thinking. The radical Protestant tradition, and in particular the tradition of dissent, emerged as a consequence of the new clerical regulations introduced by the Act of Uniformity in 1662 and the Act of Toleration in 1689, discussed above. These legal measures resulted in a dramatic rise in the number of dissenting groups during the eighteenth century. And perhaps most importantly, as Rix points out, "Blake wrote at a time when the Evangelical Revival [of the Church of England] had profoundly changed the religious landscape and public life in England, encompassing a recovery of spiritual vigour and philanthropic compassion for the poor and needy" (105).

Blake's Religion

Perhaps the most stereotyped conception of any Blake issue has traditionally been his religious background. At least, that is how it used to be. According to this view, Blake's background unquestionably was of non-conformist dissent. It was taken more or less for granted that Blake's family was quite radical and that they gave their son an upbringing that fit these opinions. Concomitantly, from this assumption commentators simply derived that Blake must naturally have acquired highly radical and dissenting religious beliefs.

This outmoded view is now strongly contested by Keri Davies, with the basis in his crucial findings of Blake's mother's Moravian background:

> If we examine the contexts that could have exerted an influence on the young, maturing, Blake, they are likely to have originated in Moravian practices typified by what could be found in Fetter Lane. While Blake's entry into adulthood and the turbulent years of the French Revolution may have made him break from his mother's influence, it is quite clear that in many ways Moravian beliefs or practices formed the core of his background. Moravianism, I would argue, "marked" Blake, and has left its recoverable traces on his work ["The Winepress of Love," 8].

However, the Moravian background being such a recent finding, the most common view of Blake is as a Swedenborgian, something that Robert Rix also confirms: "In a study of Blake's religious influences, Swedenborgianism is one of the first and most obvious starting points" (47). This is even established by evidence — the only proof of its kind that we have — in the form of the signatures of William and Catherine Blake participating in the Swedenborgian conference at Great East Cheap in 1789.[1] On that occasion he and his wife were among the seventy-seven subscribers to the beliefs of Emanuel Swedenborg and eighteen founders of the New Jerusalem Church that made a clear-cut break with the Old Church. The meeting had been called specifically for this purpose: to create the New

Jerusalem Church which was to break completely with the Old Church, in response to a circular letter a few months earlier. Forty-two propositions for the doctrinal terms to separate from the Old Church were included in the letter and it was a prerequisite for all the delegates at the conference to subscribe to and sign these to be allowed to participate at the meeting. So even though there are several indications that this was not Blake's first contact with Swedenborgian circles,[2] there is no doubt he signed on and subscribed to the forty-two propositions and at least for part of the time attended the conference.

It has further been assumed that Blake only a little later completely broke with the doctrines of Swedenborg. This breech is believed to have taken place around the time of writing the supposedly satirical *Marriage of Heaven and Hell* (which was, as we know, a travesty on Swedenborg's *Heaven and Hell*) in the first few years of the 1790s. But as I will demonstrate, although Blake admittedly questioned certain key concepts of Swedenborg, there was never a definite break with Swedenborgianism. For instance, in *Milton* Blake positively describes Swedenborg as the "strongest of men, the Samson shorn by the Churches" (22: 50, E 117). And in his *Descriptive Catalogue* from 1809, Blake notices that "the works of this visionary are worthy the attention of Painters and Poets" (E 546). Again, Rix provides support, indicating Blake's ambivalent and complex attitude to the Swedish theological philosopher: "Swedenborg remained an inspiration, and an opponent, who helped Blake to clarify his own position as a religious thinker" (65). Rather, being a sceptic by nature, at the same time as he was still embracing its most progressive ideas, Blake in later life kept a sound distance from the most dogmatic, and in his view questionable, core of the philosophy. This core element was mainly quite patriarchal, something that Blake instinctively disliked and contested. Therefore, Blake's view of Swedenborg was allegedly quite mixed, as some of Blake's closest friends could confirm: "According to Dr. J. J. Garth Wilkinson, Blake informed Tulk that he had two different states; one in which he liked Swedenborg's writings, and one in which he disliked them" (James Spilling, "Blake the Visionary," *New Church Magazine*, VI [1887], 210; quoted in Paley, "A New Heaven," 82). This is also roughly how Rix interprets Blake's relation to Swedenborg, as he usefully points to Blake's changing opinions in his annotations of the Swedish prophet's work, from scarce comments to *Heaven and Hell* in 1784, by far the most positive opinions about *Divine Love and Wisdom* in 1788, and downright rejection of *Divine Providence* in 1790 — significantly, the time of the creation of *The Marriage* (Rix, 49).

Inevitably, as we can gather from above, Blake's relation to Swedenborgianism has always caused quite some controversy in Blake studies, and critics have often seemed to be of two minds as to how to interpret this issue. One of many such commentators is Mark Schorer: "The striking fact about his use of Swedenborg is that he derived ... the materials for his myth from the dogma that he rejected" (122). A very telling remark, which certainly does not solve the problem but only poses new questions. Why, for instance, would Blake use parts of a dogma that he supposedly rejected and insert them into his own myth in order to get his important, but notoriously difficult, message through to his readers?

Therefore, if we avoid over-interpreting these very few quite vague inklings, why cannot the case quite simply be that Blake had, if not a traditional Christian upbringing, at least a Moravian one not that distant from the Church of England, and that his more deviant religious ideas came in mature age and as a result stayed with him for the rest of his life? This has been one of the main indications emanating from Keri Davies's discovery of the Moravian roots of Blake's family. In a recent paper presented at the "Blake at 250" conference in York, Davies convincingly demonstrates that, firstly, Blake's family was not one of radical dissent, and secondly, that certain documents and ceremonial events point either directly or indirectly to the Moravians. By scrutinizing the translation of Henry Crabb Robinson's well-known 1811 essay on Blake in German, "William Blake, Künstler, Dichter und religiöser Schwärmer," so seminal to subsequent Blake studies, Davies proves that by a slight misinterpretation of the connotations of the two key-words "Dissentierende" and "Gemeinde" Blake scholars have ever since then been misled to believe that Blake was born into a radical dissenting family. The full entry reads: "Jedoch gehört Blake nicht zur bischöflichen Kirche, sondern von Geburt zu einer dissentirenden Gemeinde, obgleich wir nicht glauben, dass er sich regelmässig zu irgend einer christlichen Kirche halte"[3] (Henry Crabb Robinson, "William Blake, Künstler"). The crunch word here is "Gemeinde," which traditionally has been rather sloppily retranslated back into English as "community"—for instance by Bentley in his Blake biography *The Stranger from Paradise*. "Gemeinde" is difficult to translate into English, but since the translation reads "community" and not, which would be the natural for a follower of a recognized dissenting church, "sect" or "congregation," it raises a few eyebrows. As Davies rightly stresses, "community" is a word with a strong Moravian connotation, which originates in a new type of religious community developed by the Moravians in the mid–eighteenth century. The original word, an archaic German form, was "Gemeine," which takes in all the separate meanings of congregation, community and church. Through Moravian practice it acquired the meaning of religious settlement, or closed community.[4] Another misleading term in Crabb Robinson's entry is "bischöflischer Kirche." To fully correspond to Crabb Robinson's likely original, "established church," it should have been translated as "Staatskirche" (Davies, "The Winepress of Love," 1–2). From all this we have a fairly clear-cut case of Blake's family more likely being of Moravian influence than being radical dissenters. The question that we need to ask, rather, is who and what made Blake become a Swedenborgian?

Perhaps the best place to begin a discussion of religion in Blake is with his two short philosophical and polemical companion tractates "All Religions Are One" and "There Is No Natural Religion." Not only were these his first works in illuminated writing, but, more significantly, they were created at the crucial time when we can assume that Blake was at the peak of his interest in the theology of Emanuel Swedenborg. Produced in 1788, a year before *Songs of Innocence,* the two small volumes were also the first to evidently use his dualistic/dialectical doctrine.

Just like *Songs of Innocence and of Experience*, the "Religion" tractates should be read in juxtaposition. If they are, they demonstrate many of the central tenets of Blake's lifelong philosophy. Most vital is his belief that man is the true visionary, the Poetic Genius. This he posits as the first principle of "All Religions": "That the Poetic Genius is the true Man" (E 1). From this follows that God is in every man, which is the core of Blake's religious belief: "God becomes as we are, that we may be as he is" ("There Is No Natural Religion"[b], E 3). Inevitably then, all human beings are equal: all religions are one. With such a humanist basic view, we can easily realize why Blake remained an advocate of equality throughout his life.

The second important lesson we can learn about Blake's religious outlook from the tractates is his strong and constant distrust of all organized forms of religion, particularly state religion. Paradoxically, it also gives some idea of why Blake discontinued his engagement with the newly formed Swedenborg church after its foundational conference in 1789. There is good reason to assume that, for one thing, he found it too organized and conservative for his taste and chose to be officially on the outside of the church.

Quite naturally the fervor of Blake's commitment to Swedenborg shifted in the years to come, as Morton Paley has explained in his seminal essay "'A New Heaven Is Begun': Blake and Swedenborgianism."

> The nature of Blake's interest in Swedenborg can, moreover, be divided into four distinct periods. From the late 1780s until 1790, Blake's attitude was studious and respectful; even in disagreeing with Swedenborg during these years, Blake expresses himself so as to put the most optimistic construction upon Swedenborg's doctrines. In 1790 Blake repudiated Swedenborg vehemently in the marginalia to *Divine Providence,* and he wrote at least part of the satire of *The Marriage of Heaven and Hell.* From 1793, when *The Marriage* was completed, to about 1800 there is little to indicate interest in Swedenborg on Blake's part; but after 1800 Swedenborgian concepts and references began to reappear in Blake's works, and in 1809 he exhibited a picture on a Swedenborgian subject. In this late period Blake's view of Swedenborg tends to be ambivalent... [64–5].

Following the lead of Morton Paley, it has been an almost unanimous belief in Blake circles that Blake abandoned his Swedenborgian ideas shortly after the 1789 conference and at once became very critical of his former religious inspiration. It is also commonly stated that Blake to some degree returned to Swedenborgian tenets later in his life, perhaps twenty years on from the alleged immersion at East Cheap. Paley is one of those commentators: "Swedenborg was much in Blake's thoughts in the nineteenth century, sometimes as a source of ideas and of subject matter, sometimes as a promulgator of ideas to be opposed, but in either respect as a powerful intellectual source" ("A New Heaven," 82). Somewhat in contradiction to Paley's view, as I have already mentioned, I believe that Blake retained his interest in Swedenborgianism even after 1790. The early years of the 1790s were very productive years to Blake and not only did he develop and refine his unique illuminated writing technique, but he also filled his *Notebook* with many often quite haunting poems. Some of these reveal an astonishingly frank attitude towards sex and relations and show a poet uncertain about some key notions of and not sure of which direction to take with his Swedenborgian inclination. He questioned and tested a whole number of ideas and philosophies. Moreover, it is striking that many of the *Notebook* poems were written around the same time as *The Marriage*, which they seemingly contradict on many points.

The *Notebook* poems are rewarding in many aspects, and it is remarkable that they have been so rarely examined by scholars. They provide good comments on several topics, not least religion and sex, so I will have good reason to return to them for my later chapter on sexuality. Now, however, it is my purpose to investigate the religious content of the poems in order to establish to what extent they lay bare Blake's Swedenborgian and Moravian orientation.

By discussing sexual issues, the *Notebook* poems naturally also make comments on Blake's religious beliefs since sexuality, as we have already seen, was a fundamental component to both Moravian and Swedenborgian life. I will therefore start by looking at two poems that take in both of these issues, "The Garden of Love" and "I Saw a Chapel all of Gold." Both are part of a remarkable sequence of six, or even seven, poems which seemingly form some sort of argument, with love as its chief theme.

"The Garden of Love" is the fifth in succession in the *Notebook* and is the first draft of the poem of the same title that ended up in the *Songs of Experience*. The speaker, to his great dismay, finds that a chapel has been built to joy's despair in the green where he used to play. Inevitably, this is one of Blake's well-known harsh criticisms of the church as a restricting and hostile institution, which becomes obvious by the negative use of the familiar words from the Ten Commandments in the second stanza: "And the gates of the chapel were shut / And 'thou shalt not' writ over the door" (5–6). This impression is emphasized in the next and final stanza, where the speaker/Blake blames the church and its representatives for destroying what is innocent, naturally lively and filled with happiness:

> And I saw it was filled with graves
> And tomb stones where flowers should be,
> And priests in black gounds were walking their rounds
> And binding with briars my joys & desires [9–12].

Here, and elsewhere in his poetry, Blake is quick to single out the priests of the state church as the main perpetrators in this issue. It is significant that neither among the Moravians nor the Swedenborgians (to the extent they existed among the latter) did priests have such a repulsive and unsympathetic function and influence on their congregation, so the word and its synonyms did not have a negative connotation.

The sixth and final poem in this cluster, "I Saw a Chapel all of Gold," is even more remarkable in its clever combination of two important issues: sex and religion. Here again we encounter the barred chapel "That none did dare to enter in" (2, E 467), but in this poem the sexual connotations of certain symbols cannot be ignored on any level of interpretation. The key symbol, the serpent, clearly contains both the sexual and the religious sphere, and there is no doubt that the outcome of the poem is, again, a severe critique of the latter. For one thing, the serpent naturally takes us back to the temptation and sin of the Garden of Eden. The great temptation and deceiver, here also representing the penis, is prevented from entering the church, here also denoting the female genitalia. Despite the prohibition, the serpent "Down the golden hinges tore" (9, E 467). Advancing in all his length along the aisle (the vagina) the serpent (the penis) forces himself all the way up to the altar (the bottom of the vagina), "Vomiting his poison out" (14, E 467) (ejaculating). To fulfill the forceful condemnation of the church as repressive institution this is significantly done "On the bread & on the wine" (15, E 467). This certainly must be one of Blake's most emphatic accusations of the church.

The next two poems, "I Asked a Thief" and "I Heard an Angel Singing," are noteworthy because of the inclusion of this typically Swedenborgian figure, the angel. In Swedenborgian theology there were even different orders, a bit like ranks, of angels. For them the angel was always a good figure, a representation of deceased persons in the afterlife. Significantly, in *Heaven & Hell* Swedenborg writes that "[t]he best angels of all go naked" (44), emphasizing the good-natured quality of the angels. He even, somewhat contradictorily, spoke of "angelic sexual love," something which demonstrates his belief that we all simply continue our mundane life after we have died, taking the everyday components with us to another level. "I asked a Thief" is a continuation on the love-theme, with angelic overtones. In a playful mood, a benevolent angel intrudes in the second stanza as a substitute for the speaker in order to rescue the situation and help showing the poet the feasibility of naturally fulfilling one's sexual desires—catching joy as it flies, as it were:

> As soon as I went an angel came:
> He wink'd at the thief
> And smil'd at the dame
> And without one word said
> Had a peach from the tree,

> And still as a maid
> Enjoy'd the Lady [5–11, E 468–69].

The sexual act of taking the lady's virginity is quite swiftly and impulsively done; there is no time to waste for talking. Clearly, this is one of Swedenborg's good angels, who works to promote innocent sexuality and overthrow the restrictive decrees of the Bible. If they are ripe, fruits (of love) are there to be enjoyed. Notably, the angel is a male, Blake again indicating the need for gender collaboration to achieve success.

"I Heard an Angel Singing" somewhat resembles a skeletal forerunner to "The Divine Image" of *Innocence*, with its repetition of Mercy, Pity and Peace. Or, even more so, it seems that Blake brought these three virtues from the finished poem in order to make the contrast which was eventually to be "The Human Abstract" of *Experience*. Significantly, it is a devil who recites the lines which were to end up in this poem:

> Mercy could be no more
> If there was nobody poor
> And pity no more could be
> If all were as happy as we [11–14, E 470].

Obviously a poem not fully thought-through, "I Heard an Angel Singing" underscores Blake's central tenet of contraries, with an angel again assuming a strikingly positive function. Where but in Swedenborg could Blake have found inspiration for this?

A poem which displays the most fundamental of Christian principles, the forgiveness of sins, is "Christian Forbearance," the forerunner to the *Experience* poem "A Poison Tree." As we know, this would become one of the most important components of *Jerusalem*. At this point in Blake's life the pre-eminence of this idea, also seen in the "Mercy, Pity and Peace" of the above poem, is more noteworthy than when he voiced it as a mature man in his fifties and sixties. It seems to come quite naturally to him, and consequently one is curious about its source here. Could it be traced back to his Moravian background, with their great emphasis on the Christ figure?

A little further on in the *Notebook* we come across one of those religiously based negations, Nobodaddy. This God-figure, in essence, represents the opposite of the humanitarian forgiveness of Jesus; this is a jealous and avenging God, the "Father of Jealousy" (2, E 471). Nobodaddy, nobody's daddy, is the lawgiving Jehovah of the Ten Commandments, who is sooner to punish than to forgive, the basic characteristics of what shortly was to become Urizen. In "To Nobodaddy" Blake seems to link this negativity to the female:

> Why darkness & obscurity
> In all thy words and laws
> That none dare eat the fruit but from
> The wily serpents jaws?
> Or is it because Secresy gains females' loud applause? [5–9, E 471].

Whatever the reasons for Blake's disillusionment with the female sex at this point in his life, it appears to have been profound since the next insertion in the *Notebook* is the first draft of "The Lilly," which together with "My Pretty Rose-tree" and "Ah! Sunflower!" forms the most poignant plate from *Songs of Experience* to deal with this subject. These poems will be discussed in the chapter, "Blake's Sexuality."

There are a few more *Notebook* entries worth our attention, repeating the messages of the ones that we have already discussed, which could be related to Swedenborgian or Moravian concepts. This goes for "The Little Vagabond," "Holy Thursday" and "The Angel," to name the most evident examples. But since these focus on ideas similar to those just investigated, I will leave them for the time being and move on in Blake's poetic production.

First a step back in time, though, to the *Songs of Innocence*. We need to take a closer look at a few of the key symbols in that collection. Particularly pertinent to our discussion is "The Lamb." This meek and humble animal is a key symbol for the Moravians, signifying their spirituality. The lamb is a frequent inclusion in the Moravian hymns. The following is a significant example:

> 1   HOLY Lamb, and Prince of Peace,
> Hear my Soul implore Thy Grace,
> Let it thro' Thy Pow'r divine,
> In Thy Lamb-like Meekness shine.
> 2   Grant, that faithfully I may
> As a Lamb Thy Voice obey,
> Soul and Body brought with Price,
> Be Thy living Sacrifice.
> 3   Valiant, stedfast may my Love
> In the hardest Tryals prove;
> And in all Adversity,
> Both a Lamb and Lion be.

> 4   Keep Thou me a feeble Child,
> Sober, watchful, undefil'd;
> That where'er Thy Steps I see,
> Simply I may follow Thee.
> 5   Thou the great victorious Lamb,
> Who all Hosts of Hell o'ercame;
> Grant, that in Thy Blood I may
> Conqu'ror be till Thy great Day.
> 6   When Thou shalt on Sion stand,
> I shall be at Thy Right-Hand;
> In Thy God-like Glory bright,
> Thou my Temple, Thou my Light.[5]

Like "The Lamb" this hymn deals with the Christian paradox of the "great, victorious Lamb." And instead of Blake's lamb and tiger we here have a Lamb and a Lion.

Another relevant Moravian hymn is "Hail, O Jesu, sweet and mild":

Hail, my Jesus, sweet and mild;
Hail thou holy humble Child;
Thou didst give thy self for me,
Lo! I give my self to Thee[6] [Davies, "Blake and Moravianism" 9–10].

Again, we can observe striking resemblances of both theme and vocabulary to "The Lamb":

> He is called by thy name,
> For he calls himself a Lamb:
> He is meek & he is mild,
> He became a little child:
> I a child & thou a lamb,
> We are called by his name" [13–16, E 9].

Hence, "The Lamb," and possibly the rest of *Songs of Innocence*, is most likely not the simplistic and straightforward poem it has always been made out to be by all sorts of commentators. Of course, for poetic structure and on the superficial level it is fair to say that it is in fact a simple poem, but if we see to its potential background it becomes a far more challenging issue. Indeed, if, as is probable, Blake took inspiration in Moravian hymnody then more has to be read into the *Songs* than has previously and traditionally been believed. Particularly, that goes for the *Innocence* poems, which may show more levels than what are known today.

A challenging poem in the *Experience* collection is "To Tirzah." For one thing, it clearly demonstrates Blake's great Biblical knowledge:

> Whate'er is Born of Mortal Birth
> Must be consumed with the Earth
> To rise from Generation free:
> Then what have I to do with thee? [1–4, E 30].

Tirzah, like Rahab, was imported unconditionally by Blake directly from the Bible. Together with Vala and Enitharmon these two are the most negative of the female characters in Blake's poetry. Sexuality is their domain, where Rahab is the whore and Tirzah the prude. Somewhat like Vala and Enitharmon the two work in tandem, concocting delusive strategies to entice the male sex. Furthermore, we probably have a Moravian reference in this poem too, bearing in mind the Moravians' strong focus on the crucifixion:

> The Death of Jesus set me free:
> Then what have I to do with thee? [14–15, E 30].

By the time Blake sets out on the creation of his three majestic, long prophetic poems, often referred to as epics, a lot has changed in his approach to art and poetry. After the critically alleged turn in his philosophy around the mid 1790s he focused his artistic energy on promoting improved equality between the sexes, a brotherhood-like togetherness and a forgiveness of sins in line with the preaching of Jesus, with a previously unacknowledged Moravian impetus. The other major addition is, of course, the significantly expanded and now quite coherent mythological system. While all the new symbols and characters greatly enhance the poetry of Blake they also lend it a new obscurity and opacity, which makes it extra difficult interpret and to penetrate to the very core. This may naturally be Blake's intention, but it certainly does not make the task of the literary critic any easier. In my opinion, one of the issues that suffers the most from the additional obstacles of mystery and arcane delight is religion, and in comparison I find it considerably easier to single out components pertaining to sexuality and gender relations from the three great prophecies.

In spite of this, I will attempt to make some comments on Blake's treatment of religious matters in these poems. To a large extent Blake's use of religion in the epics is centered on his particular rendition of the apocalypse, and I will therefore stick to these sections in my investigation. The longest and most rewarding apocalyptic section is to be found in *The Four Zoas*, so it is here I will start, which is only natural since it is the first in sequence.

We see the first signs of apocalypse in the eighth night of the *Zoas*. The initial portent of the revelation to come is the creation of a universal female character, Jerusalem:

> Thus forming a Vast family wondrous in beauty & love
> And they appeard a Universal female form created
> From those who were dead in Ulro from the spectres of the dead
> And Enitharmon namd the Female Jerusalem the holy
> Wondring she saw the Lamb of God within Jerusalem's Veil
> The Divine Vision seen within the inmost deep recess
> Of fair Jerusalem's bosom in a gently beaming fire [8: 187–193, E 376].

When Jerusalem appears Albion has found his counterpart and through the potential union the poem can now move towards its resolution. Praise is quickly proclaimed as the Lamb of God "now beginneth to put off the dark Satanic body / Now we behold redemption" (8: 196–97, E 376).

The character Jerusalem has a vital function already in *The Four Zoas*. She is the one to discover the dead body of Christ. She then takes the body down from the cross and buries it in a sepulchre with the assistance of Los:

Los took the Body from the Cross Jerusalem weeping over
They bore it to the Sepulcher which Los had hewn in the rock
Of Eternity for himself he hewd it despairing of Life Eternal [8: 338–40, E 379].

So again we see that the importance of the Christ figure is emphasized in Blake, now significantly in connection with the apocalypse. Can this unique scene in English literature be one of those indicating a strong Moravian influence?

Now that Blake has clearly announced the apocalyptic intention of *The Four Zoas* there are several manifestations and harbingers of what is to come in the text. To begin with, Enion announces that "the time of love / Appears upon the rocks & hills" (8: 538–39, E 384). The negative aspects of all individuals, the Spectres, are annihilated: "For I am now surrounded by a shadowy vortex drawing / The Spectre quite away from Enion that I die a death / Of bitter hope" (8: 545–47, E 384). With the extinction of the negations a superior existence materializes as "the time approaches fast … When the man gently fades away in his immortality / When the mortal disappears in improved knowledge cast away / The former things" (8: 549–53, E 384–85).

But again there is a strong emphasis on Christ as the initiator of apocalypse through the Second Coming: "The Lamb of God has rent the Veil of Mystery soon to return / In Clouds & Fires around the rock & the Mysterious tree" (8: 556–57, E 385). Man must return to an innocence similar to original Paradise in order to avoid the conflicts of the fallen world:

> And in the cries of birth & in the groans of death his voice
> Is heard throughout the Universe whereever a grass grows
> Or a leaf buds The Eternal Man is seen is heard is felt
> And all his Sorrows till he reassumes his ancient bliss [8: 580–83, E 385].

This state of higher innocence can only be accomplished through the Second Coming of Christ. Therefore Los and Enitharmon must take down Christ's body from the cross, so that he can rise again:

> And Los & Enitharmon took the Body of the Lamb
> Down from the Cross & placd it in a Sepulcher which Los had hewn
> For himself in the Rock of Eternity trembling & in despair
> Jerusalem wept over the Sepulcher two thousand years [8: 593–96, E 385].

This is also an important passage of gender politics, since, significantly, this symbolic action is performed by man and woman together.

At the beginning of the final night of *The Four Zoas* the presence of Christ becomes even more crucial, in what seems to be a Moravian passage. As the construction of the celestial city of Jerusalem starts Los and Enitharmon weep "over the Crucified body" (9: 1–2, E 386). Los gathers strength for his impending apocalyptic work through the spiritual inspiration of Christ: "But Jesus stood beside them in the Spirit Separating / Their Spirit from their body" (9: 4–5, E 386). He is now ready to end earthly existence:

> Los his vegetable hands
> Outstretchd his right hand branching out in fibrous Strength
> Siezd the Sun. His left hand like dark roots coverd the Moon
> And tore them down cracking the heavens across from immense
>   to immense [9: 6–9, E 386].[7]

After this magnificent passage, Blake reverts to the use of more traditional Biblical symbols:

> Then fell the fires of Eternity with loud & shrill
> Sound of Loud Trumpet thundering along from heaven to heaven

> A mighty sound articulate Awake ye dead & come
> To judgment from the four winds Awake & Come away [9: 10–13, E 386].

In this section of the poem Blake is evidently influenced by the classical descriptions of the apocalypse in the Bible:

> Folding like scrolls of the Enormous volume of Heaven & Earth
> With thunderous noise & dreadful shakings rocking to & fro
> The Heavens are shaken & the Earth removed from its place
> The foundations of the Eternal hills discoverd [9: 12–17, E 386–87].

Notably, there is much in common here with the long apocalypse in Isaiah:

> [F]or the windows from on high are open, and the foundations of the earth do shake. The earth is utterly broken down, the earth is clean dissolved, the earth is moved exceedingly. The earth shall reel to and fro like a drunkard, and shall be removed like a cottage; and the transgression thereof shall be heavy upon it; and it shall fall, and not rise again [24: 18–20, 713].

Similar, but less striking, lines are to be found in Revelation 11: 19. With a few more effective lines of upheaval Blake finishes the first apocalyptic section of *The Four Zoas*:

> The thrones of Kings are shaken they have lost their robes & crowns
> The poor smite their oppressors they awake up to the harvest
> The naked warriors rush down to the sea shore
> Trembling before the multitudes of slaves now set at liberty
> They are become like wintry flocks like forests stripd of leaves
> The oppressed pursue like the wind there is no room for escape
>   [9: 18–23, E 387].

Significantly, Blake makes good use of the typically Moravian symbol of the Lamb in the last apocalyptical night of *The Four Zoas*. What may otherwise be seen as a surprising choice of traditional Biblical imagery instead becomes a sign of Blake's unusual religious background. For instance, flocks of woolly lambs appear after Luvah and Vala have descended to earth. For Blake the lamb is an ambiguous symbol, not only representing the Moravian association with Christ but is also manifesting the innocence of Blake's utopia: "I walk among his flocks & hear the bleating of his lambs" (9: 425, E 396). The innocence and the soft quality of the lamb are underscored further as Vala intends to erect a house in Beulah to function as a place of rest: "So spoke the sinless soul & laid her head on the downy fleece / Of a curld Ram who stretchd himself in sleep beside his mistress" (9: 455–56, E 397).

The interlude episode known as "Vala's Garden" is the final launch of apocalypse in *The Four Zoas*. Soon after we have left the pastoral idyll of Beulah behind, Blake's definite negation Urizen to his immense satisfaction announces that "Times are Ended" (9: 568, E 400). With this commences the concluding apocalyptic section of *The Four Zoas*:

> This sickle Urizen took the scythe his sons embracd
> And went forth & began to reap & all his joyful sons
> Reapd the wide Universe & bound in Sheaves a wondrous harvest
> They took them into the wide barns with loud rejoicings & triumph
> Of flute & harp & drum & trumpet horn & clarion
> The feast was spread in the bright South & the Regenerate Man
> Sat at the feast rejoicing & the wine of Eternity
> Was servd round by the flames of Luvah all Day & all the Night
>   [9:582–89, E 400].

By introducing a new kind of imagery related to harvest — "sickle," "scythe," "reap," "Sheaves," "wondrous harvest," "wide barns" — Blake indicates that the poem is drawing towards its close with the human harvest of the subsequent consummation of the apocalypse.

Further towards the end we are again reminded of the child-like innocent quality that we saw represented by the Moravian symbol of the Lamb. In these lines Blake approximates the simple language of the *Songs of Innocence*, particularly "The Lamb":

> Then shall they lift their innocent hands & stroke his furious nose
> And he shall lick the little girls white neck & on her head
> Scatter the perfume of his breath while from his mountains high
> The lion of terror shall come down & bending his bright mane
> And couching at their side shall eat from the curld boys white lap
> His golden food and in the evening sleep before the Door [9: 703–08, E 403].

This passage is also a Biblical echo from Isaiah: "The wolf and the lamb shall feed together, and the lion shall eat straw like the bullock" (65: 25, 748).

In the concluding apocalyptical lines of *The Four Zoas* Blake completely casts off the negative implications of religion, "the dark Religions," in favor of a perfect existence of intellect and art in the reigning "sweet Science" of futurity:

> And the fresh Earth beams forth ten thousand thousand springs of life
> Urthona is arisen in his strength no longer now

> Divided from Enitharmon no longer the spectre Los
> Where is the Spectre of Prophecy where the delusive Phantom
> Departed & Urthona rises from the ruinous walls
> In all his ancient strength to form the golden armour of science
> For intellectual War The war of swords departed now
> The dark Religions are departed & sweet Science reigns [9: 848–55, E 407].

In many respects *Milton* is a different kind of poem, compared both to *The Four Zoas* and *Jerusalem*. For one thing, it is not, like the other two major prophecies, a fully apocalyptic poem. Secondly, it is a personal poem in which Blake in a symbolic form makes unusual comments on his current domestic life. These are two reasons that *Milton* does not lend itself to an examination of religious issues as easily as *The Four Zoas* and *Jerusalem*. It will therefore be dealt with more briefly here and I will, again, restrict myself to remarks on the (pre-) apocalyptic section near the end of the poem.

Like in *The Four Zoas* and *Jerusalem* the reawakening of everyman Albion is the main symbolic indicator in *Milton* that the apocalypse is drawing near. At the end of the first book there are signs of arousal in Albion: "Now Albions sleeping Humanity began to turn upon his Couch; / Feeling the electric flame of Miltons awful precipitate descent" (20: 25–26, E 114). Significantly, this moment occurs just after the character Milton has resisted the temptations of several alluring hermaphroditic women in the previous plate. This is a positive sign, but Albion will not fully wake up until Milton is reunited with his emanation, Ololon.

However, already in plate 18 we can find the first signs of the imminent apocalypse. On this plate a number of apocalyptic images are introduced in a passage anticipating the pre-apocalyptic finish of *Milton*:

> Thus darkend the Shadowy Female tenfold & Orc tenfold
> Glowd on his rocky Couch against the darkness: loud thunders
> Told of the enormous conflict[.] Earthquake beneath: around;
> Rent the Immortal Females, limb from limb & joint from joint
> And moved the fast foundations of the Earth to wake the Dead
> [18: 46–50, E 112].

We can easily here recognize a few Biblical symbols from *The Four Zoas*: "darkness," "loud thunders," "earthquake." But since there are fewer apocalyptic passages in *Milton* than in *The Four Zoas* and *Jerusalem*, the poem is not as pregnant with Biblical symbolism.

Instead of traditional Biblical apocalyptic symbols, in *Milton* Blake makes use of other harbingers of apocalypse. One such good example is the lark, which soars to the sky in plate 31:

> The lark sitting upon his earthy bed: just as the morn
> Appears; listens silent; then springing from the waving Cornfield! loud
> He leads the Choir of Day! trill, trill, trill, trill,
> Mounting upon the wings of light into the Great Expanse:
> Reechoing against the lovely blue & shining heavenly Shell:
> His little throat labours with inspiration; every feather
> On throat & breast & wings vibrates with the effluence Divine
>   [31: 29–35, E 130].

The lark is a standard symbol of the advent of apocalypse. The significance of the passage becomes even clearer as we also find another traditional apocalyptic omen, "The Wild Thyme" (31: 51, E 131), further on in the same plate.

There is a slight Biblical echo near the end of *Milton* when all the four zoas appear, blowing the "Four Trumpets" (42: 23, E 143) that announce the apocalypse. The advent of the four zoas, being aspects of Albion, is a signal for mankind to awake in time for apocalypse. Notably, at this point, lending a Moravian touch to the poem, Jesus appears. Since *Milton* is a rather autobiographical poem, Blake links the advent of Christ to his personal sphere as "Jesus wept & walked forth / From Felpham's Vale clothed in Clouds of blood" (42: 19–20, E 143). The mentioning of blood in relation to Christ naturally makes this a remarkably Moravian passage in Blake's poetry. Jesus then goes on "to enter into / Albion's Bosom" (42: 20–21, E 143), as a sign of the ultimate reunion before apocalypse.

In *Jerusalem* it is the eponymous and main female character who leads the poem towards apocalypse. In the final plates Blake cunningly makes Jerusalem, the Woman merge with Jerusalem, the City. Jerusalem descends from heaven as a City, yet a Woman; a Biblical idea found in Ezekiel and Revelation. In Revelation the corresponding passage reads: "And I John saw the holy city, new Jerusalem, coming down from God out of heaven, prepared as a bride adorned for her husband" (21: 2, 1234). Morton Paley develops the idea of double signification in *The Continuing City:* "The common elements are a woman (yet a city) who exists in illo tempore in a state of primal innocence, who is then rejected as a sexual transgressor, and who is elevated in her regenerate form as the mother of us all" (180).

The main difference between the apocalyptic sections in *The Four Zoas* and *Jerusalem* is that in the latter poem there is no obvious preparation for the apocalypse in the form of various symbolic premonitions. Instead, there is quite an abrupt inception and in plate 94 the apocalypse suddenly begins. The only foreboding we are presented with is the indication that the sleeping Albion is about to wake up at the end of the previous plate: "Is it not that Signal of the Morning which was told us in the Beginning" (93: 26, E 254). Then, in the next plate it is announced that conventional time is ended:

> Time was Finished! The Breath Divine Breathed over Albion
> Beneath the Furnaces & starry Wheels and in the Immortal Tomb
> And England who is Brittannia awoke from Death on Albions bosom
>   [94: 18–20, E 254].

After this initiation, the remaining six plates of *Jerusalem* deal with the apocalypse, in text as well as in illustrations.

The chief poetic improvement in *Jerusalem* is the use of more effective imagery. This makes the apocalypse shorter and more concentrated than in *The Four Zoas*. Even though we can recognize the symbols from the *Zoas*, in *Jerusalem* Blake combines the purely utopian images with those more clearly denoting gender interactivity:

> [I]nto the Heavens he walked clothed in flames
> Loud thundring, with broad flashes of flaming lightning & pillars
> Of fire, speaking the Words of Eternity in Human Forms, in direful
> Revolutions of Action & Passion [95: 7–10, E 255].

If we take "Revolutions" to mean movement, Blake is here underscoring the need for both action and movement to advance further towards apocalypse.

As in *The Four Zoas* it is obvious in *Jerusalem* that the key concepts for the Blakean apocalypse are unity and togetherness. While there are conventional apocalyptic signifiers similar to the symbols in *The Four Zoas*—"Furnaces," "Fountains," "soft clouds," "flaming fires"—in *Jerusalem* there is a more intense drive towards unity as the four zoas reappear in pursuit of their proper eternal positions in the impending fourfold vision:

> All was a Vision, all a Dream: the Furnaces became
> Fountains of Living Waters flowing from the Humanity Divine
> And all the Cities of Albion rose from their Slumbers, and All
> The Sons & Daughters of Albion on soft clouds Waking from Sleep
> Soon all around remote the Heavens burnt with flaming fires
> And Urizen & Luvah & Tharmas & Urthona arose into

> Albions Bosom: Then Albion stood before Jesus in the Clouds
> Of Heaven Fourfold among the Visions of God in Eternity
> [96: 36–43, E 256].

In *Jerusalem* the concept of vision is more compelling and fully thought-through than in the earlier poem. Perhaps this is only natural bearing in mind that Blake had gained some twenty years more experience since the first epic. However, in both poems a reunion of male and female is called for to regain paradise and Blake stresses the need for man and woman to enter Eden in togetherness. As Albion's emanation, Jerusalem therefore must also awake: "For lo! the Night of Death is past and the Eternal Day / Appears upon our Hills: Awake Jerusalem, and come away" (97: 3–4, E 256). Now it only remains for the four zoas to resume their eternal positions for lost harmony finally to be reinstated:

> And every Man stood Fourfold. each Four Faces had. One to the West
> One toward the East One to the South One to the North [98: 12–13, E 257].

In this world of ultimate fourfold harmony the level of human communication assumes previously unknown expressions:

> [T]hese are the Four Rivers of Paradise
> And the Four Faces of Humanity fronting the Four Cardinal Points
> Of Heaven going forward forward irresistible from Eternity to Eternity
> And they conversed together in Visionary forms dramatic which bright
> Redounded from their Tongues in thunderous majesty, in Visions
> In new Expanses [98: 25–30, E 257].

Compared to *The Four Zoas* there are considerably fewer Biblical references in *Jerusalem*. Instead, here Blake here relies on a more developed and effective imagery, of which the well-known metonymy above — where at the apocalyptic moment the characters "conversed together in Visionary forms dramatic"— is an excellent example. This is only one of several significant examples of Blake as a more confident and relaxed poet in *Jerusalem* than in all his preceding poetry. Perhaps the ultimate evidence of this is the use of the tempter and cause of sin, the serpent, as an extreme symbol emphasizing that all sins are now redeemed and that all negations are finally revoked: "And the all wondrous Serpent clothed in gems & rich array Humanize / In the Forgiveness of Sins according to the Covenant of Jehovah" (98: 44–45, E 258). Thus, even the great error itself is eventually human and fourfold. All negations are abolished and Blake's fourfold utopian existence is launched.

From a Moravian perspective, another crucial moment in *Jerusalem* is when Albion realizes that he is human: "[F]or Man is Love: / As God is Love" (96: 26–7, E 256). It then naturally follows that through love man is equal to God, and therefore Albion is both human and God:

> [A]lbion saw his Form
> A Man. & they conversed as Man with Man, in Ages of Eternity
> And the Divine Appearance was the likeness & similitude of Los
> [96: 5–7, E 255].

This passage may be one of the proofs of Blake's reliance on Moravian ideology in *Jerusalem*. The Christian principle of forgiveness of sins was an idea greatly emphasized by the Moravians in their attitude towards their fellow human beings. This message is reiterated throughout *Jerusalem*, something which lends the poem a greater atmosphere of harmony than *The Four Zoas*: "[N]or can Man exist but by Brotherhood" (96: 28, E 256). It could be argued that with its emphasis on brotherhood, redemption and forgiveness of sins plus the predominance of Christ and his atonement, in *Jerusalem* Blake wraps up his poetic oeuvre in a hitherto not fully accomplished Moravian fashion.

To find further substantial comments by Blake that would enlighten us about his Moravian and Swedenborgian inclinations, we have to move forward a few years. It seems that sometime during the years when *Jerusalem* was his main concern, Blake returned profoundly to Biblical motifs, both in painting and in writing. His majestic masterpiece has, as we know, been frequently examined, so my investigation will now focus on two other contemporary texts, "A Vision of the Last Judgment" and "The Everlasting Gospel." These are the last two lengthy pieces of writing that Blake did, intercepted only by *Jerusalem*.

For whatever reason, at this stage of his life one must consider Blake's religious position more traditionally Christian than one or two decades earlier. To call Blake a traditional Christian is of course not quite correct—he still repudiated every form of state church, with priests as its natural representation—but compared to his most intense Swedenborgian period there is an obvious change of tone. It becomes softer, more loving and accepting. There are, however, some remnants of his previous Moravian and Swedenborgian beliefs also in his last few works. Morton Paley gives us a hint of this: "[F]rom about the turn of the century and well into the nineteenth century, Blake displays a renewed interest in (though by no means a simple attitude towards) Swedenborg. Perhaps the most dramatic instance of this interest may be seen in Blake's *Descriptive Catalogue of 1809"* ("A New Heaven," 78). Indeed, in the *Descriptive Catalogue*, launched at Blake's fiasco exhibition, we find Blake promoting the ideas of Swedenborg as never before: "The works of this visionary are well worthy the attention of Painters and Poets; they are foundations for grand things; the reason they have not been more attended to, is, because corporeal demons have gained a predominance" (E 546).

"A Vision of the Last Judgment" is in the main a description of Blake's 1808 watercolour painting "The Last Judgment," an addition to the *Descriptive Catalogue* of his 1809 exhibition. This entry was written in 1810 in a rather dense prose. There are some interesting remarks, though. Blake refers to the Bible as inspiration and the last judgment as true vision. "This world of Imagination is the world of Eternity," he writes (69, E 555). A bit further on the idea seems somewhat Swedenborgian, when after the old heaven and earth have passed away we behold "the New Heaven & New Earth descending" (76, E 556). Further on we encounter one of the most controversial and misread lines in Blake's poetry: "In Eternity Woman is the Emanation of Man; she has No Will of her own. There is no such thing in Eternity as a Female Will" (85, E 556). First, it has to be pointed out that Blake here is strictly following the creation myth from Genesis, which clearly was in line with his increasing interest in the Bible and traditional Christianity at this point in time. In Genesis, as we know, woman was created from a body part of man in order to be his life companion. If we, as Blake, follow the analogy through to the other extreme, as it were, the afterlife, then man and woman are reunited and are as one. Hence, as much as man has no will of his own in eternity, neither has woman. Quite simply, separate and individual wills do not exist. Next, Blake can be seen to return to the Swedenborgian idea of the angel in an uncommonly explicative passage: "It is not because Angels are Holier than Men or Devils that makes them Angels, but because they do not Expect Holiness from one another, but from God only" (92–95, E 557). In this we can assume that Blake's idea of angels differs somewhat from that of Swedenborg. While the latter saw angels exclusively as the otherworldly beings that deceased men turn into, Blake obviously believes that there are angels in the mundane world too.

Blake's belief in Jesus as the only true God is even more accentuated in "The Everlasting Gospel" from 1818. Included in the *Notebook*, this long and repetitive poem contains several central conflicting opinions and questions. In fact, three of the four sections, if we follow Erdman's reconstructed suggestion of a "definite" Blake version, open with quite pertinent questions about the Jesus figure. "Was Jesus gentle, or did he / Give any marks of Gentility?" (100–101: 1–2, E 521), the first of these reads. One has to agree with Morton Paley, who in his very illuminating analysis of the poem in his master study of Blake's last works, *The Traveller in the Evening,* calls it "highly antithetical" (201) and even dissonant (188). He tells us that it was written at great speed, and continues: "A gnomic, subversive, sometimes savage reinterpretation of parts of the Gospels, shot through with references to other parts of the Bible, it gives Blake's own rendering of the character of Jesus" (179). Accordingly, the second of Blake's questions reads "Was Jesus Humble? Or did he / Give any Proofs of Humility?" (52–4: 1–2, E 518). As Paley helpfully explains, indicating one of the remaining components of Swedenborgian/Moravian thinking in Blake: "The denial of humility is part of Blake's strategy of presenting an antinomian Christ who transgressed the Law and violated all common conceptions of virtue" (183). We can only agree when Paley goes on to point to the kinship between Blake's view of Jesus in this part of the poem and of his Devil in *The Marriage*. However, most intriguingly, "The Everlasting Gospel" interrogates the idea of sin, using Jesus as the focal point:

> Was Jesus Chaste? Or did he
> Give any Lessons of Chastity?
> The morning blush'd fiery red
> Mary was found in Adulterous bed [48: 1–4, E 521].

As we will shortly see, Blake has a good personal reason to bring up the issue of adultery. That he relates it to Jesus, and thus questions the only God, will find its explanation as we move on through Blake's poetry of this period.

In Blake's later life the forgiveness of sins was the foremost principle of his poetry. We have seen this in *Jerusalem* and it forms the backbone of "The Everlasting Gospel" too. Paley confirms this view and states that it "may have been the starting point of the whole poem" (194). It is so stubbornly reiterated that after a while we start wondering if there could be a more personal motive behind it. And remarkably, I believe that there may well be. It is difficult to conclude anything from "The Everlasting Gospel" alone, but if we continue with the following poem in Keynes's order in

Complete Writings, we can actually find a few clues. One is "For the Sexes: The Gates of Paradise," which, as we know, is an adult version of the 1793 "For Children." The illustrations are the same in the later poem, but here Blake has also added a prologue, a key and an epilogue. Those are the ones of interest to us. The poem starts off by repeating the message from *Jerusalem* and "The Everlasting Gospel": "Mutual Forgiveness of each Vice / Such are the Gates of Paradise" (1–2, E 259). Again, Jehovah is condemned for writing the Law and the Christians' unmitigated acceptance of it is challenged: "O Christians, Christians! tell me Why / You rear it on your Altars high" (Prologue: 10–11, E 259). Some of the illustrations are of particular interest. In line with Blake's extolment of the female sex, the inscription of the seventh plate poignantly asks "Alas! the Female Martyr, Is She also the Divine Image?" (7, E 263). The accusation and call for revenge return in plate 12: "Does thy God, O Priest, take such vengeance as this?" (E 265). In the next plate the key idea from "The Everlasting Gospel" is repeated: "Fear & Hope are — Vision" (13, E 266). Two main ideas are alternated throughout "The Gates of Paradise": the accusing God and sexual strife, represented by woman. Blake makes more extensive comments on the illustrations in what he calls "The Keys of the Gates." This follows the same order as the plates, with its alternated messages. The foundation, as always in Blake, is with the sexual organization of the fallen world. In the afterlife an existence of equality is offered:

> When weary Man enters his Cave
> He meets his Saviour in the Grave
> Some find a Female Garment there,
> And some a Male, woven with care,
> Lest the Sexual Garments sweet
> Should grow a devouring Winding sheet [19–24, E 268].

But in fallen sexuality every woman is a representation of the sexual strife of the world:

> Thou'rt my Mother from the Womb
> Wife, Sister, Daughter, to the Tomb
> Weaving to Dreams the Sexual strife
> And weeping over the Web of Life [45–8, E 269].

The final word of the epilogue is directed "To The Accuser who is / The God of This World" (Epilogue 1–2, E 269). It is here we find the obvious reference to Blake's own life:

> Every Harlot was a Virgin once
> Nor can'st thou ever change Kate into Nan [3–4, E 269].

This is difficult to misinterpret. We know that for some years, social contacts between Blake and his wife Catherine, "Kate" in the lines above, and his sculptor friend John Flaxman and his wife Nancy, almost certainly "Nan" above, were intense. From these lines it looks very plausible indeed that Blake was tempted to have, or had, an amorous affair with Nancy Flaxman. With the intricate pattern of "The Everlasting Gospel" and "The Gates of Paradise," with the issues of sexual strife, adultery, sin, guilt, accusation of God and forgiveness of sins cleverly interweaved, I would suggest the latter. I would also claim that the uncommonly strong emphasis on forgiveness in Blake's last works indicates that it was a highly personal concern caused by many years of distress, which eventually found its outlet in the Epilogue to "The Gates of Paradise."

The sequence above is only one example of how Blake's two key issues, sex and religion, are unavoidably intertwined. Moreover, since Blake regards the world as fallen, sexual division is the underpinning of religion. To move matters forward, I will therefore now turn to Blake's Moravian, and Swedenborgian, inclined interpretation of sexuality.

Blake's Sexuality

So what does the fact that Blake was brought up in a family with a Moravian background imply about the way he treated sexuality in his art and poetry? How do his probably more mature Swedenborgian sympathies influence his writing and painting? Where and when can we notice any influence? Which of the two comes first? Or, indeed, do the two amalgamate, possibly also revealing input from other contemporary religious sources?

At the same time as the breakthrough discovery of William Blake's Moravian family background provides us with vital clues which drastically change the direction of research on Blake and give us vital aid in the interpretation of his art and poetry, it also poses a whole set of new, intriguing questions. As always with Blake and our still limited knowledge of his biography, it is not easy to find answers to these questions. Nonetheless, it is my intention in this chapter to discuss these issues with the hope that some answers to the queries above will be discernable at the end of it.

There is no doubt, however, that the Moravians have now become very important players in Blake studies. Not least is that true for Blake's sexual and gender politics. The following account from Keri Davies points to obvious similarities with Blake's ideas:

> The Moravians preached that the sexual act itself is the highest expression of spirituality. The union of man and woman embodies God's love for his people. There is no inherent sin in sex; on the contrary, sexual intercourse is a sacramental activity, a physical means of grace [*William Blake in Contexts*, 303].

Hence, that Blake's view of sexuality was deeply informed by Moravian theology is a basic presumption of the subsequent discussion. The other major premise, of course, is Blake's immersion in Swedenborgianism.

It appears that during the years from 1789, when he produced *Songs of Innocence*, to the time when he added the *Experience* poems to make a double volume, a vital change occurred in Blake's foundational values. From the manifestations of the childlike mood of *Innocence* and the unfulfilled prophecies of *The Book of Thel* from the same year there is a drastic change in attitude. However, as much as a new attitude and treatment of sexual issues is evident around the time of the addition of *Songs of Experience*, this mindset may have been with Blake a few years before that. Mary Lynn Johnson, for one, conveys the view that the *Innocence* poems may not be that innocent after all, as she remarks that "Blake takes special care to free 'innocence' of its traditional associations with sexual immaturity" (61).

Conspicuously, somehow taking the cue from Johnson, Helen Bruder succeeds in finding several sexual elements in the *Songs of Innocence*. There is the most obvious example, we have to agree, in "The Blossom" with its clear genital imagery — "swift as arrow" and "cradle narrow" (4–5, E 10) — but Bruder shrewdly finds other fitting specimens, at least of Blake's great prescient gender awareness. It is as if he were striving for gender equality already in these early poems, for instance by not specifying the sex of his child-protagonists in many of the *Songs,* like "A Cradle Song," "Infant Joy," "Nurse's Song" and "The Ecchoing Green." Furthermore, Blake never succumbs to using the distinction of traditionally gendered stereotypes of the tough and the soft, in for example "The Chimney Sweeper" and "The Little Boy Lost/Found." As Bruder elaborates on her intriguing findings: "Innocence, then, is not marked by an absence of sexual activity. Rather, it's the state evoked by Oothoon: 'Infancy, fearless, lustful, happy! nestling for delight / In laps of pleasure' (VDA 6.4–5, E 49). But what are absent are fixed and stereotypical gender roles" (Williams, 138–39).

In spite of this, there are hardly any obvious, overt manifestations of sexuality in *Songs of Innocence*, but *Thel* is an important locus for the issue of sexuality in Blake, so our investigation must start with this early illustrated poem. *The Book of Thel* provides us with the first sophisticated expression of sexuality in Blake's works, but this is a poem that still breathes of innocence. In my opinion it has more in common with the *Songs,* and then particularly *Innocence,* than with *Visions of the Daughters of Albion.* This might go against the views of earlier commentators on *Thel,* who have pointed to similarities to *Visions.* Admittedly, there are some affinities between the two poems, mainly in the basic theme, where a youthful female character moves from innocence to experience, but the differences are more abundant. The chief difference is the reaction and outcome of the main female characters to the passage between the two states, from the sexlessness of childhood to the sexualized transitional period of puberty. While Thel rather weakly succumbs to the pressures and relapses back to childhood, Oothoon, as Blake's first strong female character, transcends to the more advanced state of experience, even though this does not exactly yield her any happiness or harmony.

The mutual points between *Songs of Innocence and of Experience* and *The Book of Thel* may be easier to investigate. Most clearly these occur in the rather simple and straightforward symbolism of the poems, which is obvious both in text and illustrations. If we first look at the language and imagery in *Thel* the examples are numerous already from the beginning of the poem:

> The daughters of Mne Seraphim led round their sunny Flocks.
> All but the youngest: she in paleness sought the secret air.
> To fade away like morning beauty from her mortal day:
> Down by the river of Adona her soft voice is heard:
> And thus her gentle lamentation falls like morning dew [1: 1–5, E 3].

It is not difficult to select the words associated with innocence here: "sunny flocks," "youngest," "morning beauty," "soft voice," "gentle lamentation," "morning dew." However, there are also images with a profound resonance that anticipate the approach of a more troublesome life in experience: "paleness," "secret air," "fade away," "mortal day." As Thel enters after this introduction, the juxtaposition of innocence and experience is perpetuated, at the same time as the main character remains firmly rooted at the level of innocence throughout the poem. Her strategy, and the general mood of the poem, is inquisitive. In her innocence she is wracked with fear of the advancing experience and the inevitable decay and death of everything that follow. She tries to find an answer by questioning the lilly, the cloud, the mole and the clod of clay. "O life of this our spring! Why fades the lotus of the water / Why fade these children of the spring, born but to smile & fall?" (1: 6–7, E 3), Thel first asks the lilly of the valley. The humble lilly replies by teaching Thel about the eternal beauty of life which gives us every reason to be happy to be alive since life is renewed in the light of heaven. The lilly cannot see any reason for Thel to complain. This is more or less the outcome of all the conversations between Thel and the other creations. Thel, and humankind, should be content with their lot. All the same, Thel's central question lingers till the end of the poem: Why do we all have to die?

The only controversial feature of the poem appears at the end, as Thel enters the land of death and encounters her own future grave. A sorrow-filled voice repeats the same old questions. But still there is no answer and Thel is so frightened that she reverts back to innocence, fleeing back to "the vales of Har" (6: 22, E 6). Hence, to me, *The Book of Thel* is not so much a poem about sexuality, but a poem about life with a broader perspective. However, it must be recognized that a couple of lines at the end point forward to the immense complexity of the major prophecies and to *Visions of the Daughters of Albion*. There are also other possible, and more controversial, readings of *Thel*, which I will return to further on in the book. The polyphony of *Thel* and its several interpretations is what Bruder also implies after her examination of the poem: "A tradition of sexist scholarship fiercely criticizes her flight from maternal embodiment but Blake's account of patriarchal deployments of 'the natural' in the service of the ideological suggests that his own judgment was rather different" ("Blake and Gender Studies," 142).

To establish the resemblance between the nearly simultaneously composed *Thel* and *Songs of Innocence*, we can select almost any poem from the latter volume. Images also used in *Thel* are omnipresent: lambs, angels, clouds, insects, children, virgins, meadows, soft items, birds, flowers—the list can be made much longer. But in both poetic works there are intentions of a more sophisticated and complex use of symbols, which point towards *Experience* and the prophecies. Flowers are perhaps the most striking image here and the most relevant example from *Innocence* is probably "The Blossom":

> Merry, Merry Sparrow!
> Under leaves so green
> A happy Blossom
> Sees you swift as arrow
> Seek your cradle narrow
> Near my Bosom [1–6, E 10].

In spite of the quite obvious natural symbols that first catch the eye, there are sexual implications in some of the metaphors. The use of flowers in Blake often has a sexual undertone. "Swift as arrow" indicates the penis and the sexual activity of this organ, "seek[ing the] cradle narrow," the vagina. It seems that sexual intercourse takes place and is fully consummated, since in the final stanza we find "A happy Blossom" and a sobbing robin (9–11, E 10). Bearing the positive Moravian attitude to sexuality and their glorification of the sexual act and the genitals in mind, the poem could be an expression of this influence. Even though the message is somewhat hidden in the metaphors, it was certainly not a common thing to write about such matters in contemporary poetry at Blake's time.

In *The Book of Thel* we have the lilly of the valley. To begin with, the lilly is a flower. Moreover, if we continue along this line, the valley can of course symbolize the female genitalia. However, since there is no male counterpart, there is no activity in the poem. In Blake activity must be mutual in order to be positive and this may be a reason for the surprising and negative ending of the poem. In "The Blossom," by comparison, there is a positive ending with the post-coital harmony of the second stanza.

It is therefore difficult to make a case for *The Book of Thel* as a poem primarily about sexuality. To find more substantial imagery of a sexual kind, we have to move ahead a couple of years in Blake's production. An intriguing place to start is Blake's notebook of poems from 1793. What is immediately conspicuous is that love is the theme in so many of the poems and fragments included. We can notice this already at the beginning: the first seven inclusions are about love and the disastrous impact of sexual desire. Some of the drafts of course make their way into *Songs of Experience*. This is the case with the very first draft, "My Pretty Rose-tree." This poem carries over the flower symbolism from *The Book of Thel* and *Songs of Innocence*. The main sub-theme in the poems dealing with sexuality from this period is jealousy, and this is also the case with "My Pretty Rose-tree." It is probably even one of Blake's most well-known and most effective poems in this line of thinking. So much is said in just a few lines. It very much conveys the general impression at that time that Blake was tempted in love, if we take the speaker to represent Blake's feelings. The poem also gives a hint of the troubles in William and Catherine's marriage, as Blake turns down the offer of extramarital love: "But my rose / turn'd away with Jealousy / And her thorns were my only delight" (8–10, K 161).

Apparently the poet's/Blake's love-affair came to a fairly advanced stage, with unlucky consequences for him, as we notice in the next poem, "Never Pain to Tell thy Love," where the object of his love shies away:

> I told my love I told my love
> I told her all my heart
> Trembling, cold, in ghastly fears
> Ah, she doth depart [5–8, E 467].

The "ghastly fears" inculcated by the moral laws of society force him to stay with his "pretty rose tree" and thus lose the occasion to fulfill his passion. Instead, almost unnoticed, "A traveller came by" and the opportunity and the woman are gone (10, E 467).

The difficulties and complexities of love are described in the next poem, a draft of "The Clod and the Pebble," later to be included in *Songs of Experience,* in a typically Blakean dualistic juxtaposition of the two opposite forces of love. The clod of clay defends the unselfish nature of love, but it is the pebble that best approximates Blake's own views in this cycle of poems. The last stanza clearly harks back to Blake's desperation in the former poem:

> "Love seeketh only self to please
> "To bind another to its delight
> "Joys in another's loss of ease
> "And builds a hell in heaven's despite" [9–12, *Complete Writings*, ed. Keynes, 162].

The third line is particularly illustrative of the poet's despair.

He is taught a lesson, though, and in the following poem he meditates upon his new experience. He compares his situation to thistles and thorns who are "compeld to be chaste" (8, E 468). Still in a contemplative mood, he moves on from the river bank to a garden with a nearby chapel. This first draft of "The Garden of Love" is the first notebook poem that does not directly speak of love in a physical sense. It rather continues the moral message from "The Clod and the Pebble," indirectly pointing to the prohibitions and restrictions put on love. As always in Blake, state church is a representation of this with the shut chapel and its priests "binding with briars my joys & desires" (12, K 162–63). It is without doubt that Blake/the speaker is in the thick of a very troublesome situation.

The most challenging and daring of these poems is "I Saw a Chapel All of Gold," with its astonishingly frank symbolism. Firstly, it imports the church imagery from the previous poem. But in a reading of its sexual allusions, it is easy to substitute the chapel with the female body and in this way establish the Moravian influence on Blake at this point. As Schuchard puts it: "The vagina-womb was deliberately formed as a chapel for worship so that 'we may become Saviours in this World, Saviours of the Member of that Body ... of that little Model of a Chappel of God'"

("The 'Secret' and the 'Gift,'" 212).[1] Even though there are many who worship its beauty, it is just as forbidden as the church to enter and desecrate. The poet is one of the admirers as he suddenly sees a serpent, the penis, "rise between the white pillars of the door," the vagina (5–6, E 467). The erect penis "forcd & forcd & forcd" (7, E 467), and finally thrusts into the vagina: "Down the golden hinges tore" (9, E 467). The penis drives deeper into the vagina, "along the pavements sweet," until it gets to the bottom and ejaculates: "Vomiting his poison out / On the bread & on the wine" (14–15, E 467). But this figment of the imagination has not improved his situation and the speaker of the poem "turnd into a sty / And laid [himself] down among the swine" (16–17, E 468).

That this cycle is a downright critique of state religion, or even religion in general, is obvious in the last specimen, "I Asked a Thief to Steal Me a Peach," where the hypocritical double standards are blatantly exposed. The speaker ponders theft and adultery, but both crimes are sternly averted. To his great consternation and frustration a religious representative, an angel, swiftly comes by instead and commits these very crimes through deceptive winking and smiling. This poem is a continuation on the love-theme, with angelic overtones. In a playful mood, a benevolent angel intrudes in the second stanza substituting for the speaker in order to rescue the situation and show the poet the feasibility to naturally fulfill one's sexual desires, to catch joy as it flies, as it were:

> As soon as I went an angel came:
> He wink'd at the thief
> And smil'd at the dame
> And without one word said
> Had a peach from the tree,
> And still as a maid
> Enjoy'd the Lady [5–11, E 468–69].

The sexual act of taking the lady's virginity is quite swiftly and impulsively done; there is no time for talking. Clearly, this is one of Swedenborg's good angels, who works to promote innocent sexuality and overthrow the restrictive decrees of the Bible. If they are ripe, fruits (of love) are there to be enjoyed. Notably, the angel is a male, Blake again indicating the need for gender collaboration to achieve success. What we see here is the beginning of Blake's skeptical attitude towards Swedenborgianism, something which was to have its culmination in *The Marriage*.

When discussing angels and Swedenborg the self-evident text to turn to is *The Marriage of Heaven and Hell*. This often satirical piece of writing has traditionally been read as Blake's renunciation of Swedenborgianism. As evidence, critics have used the caricature of typically Swedenborgian angels in some of the Memorable Fancies. Blake also puts forward a univocal statement about Swedenborg: "Now hear a plain fact: Swedenborg has not written one new truth. Now hear another: he has written all the old falsehoods" (21–22, E 43). Blake portrays the angel as a negative symbol to castigate in the name of religion. This is all the more remarkable since in the works of Swedenborg angels are positive beings, mediators between our worldly existence and the afterlife. They belong to the world of spirits, which Swedenborg describes as a state between heaven and hell.

The Marriage of Heaven and Hell is not a poem explicitly dealing with sex and gender issues. Bruder writes that it "remains just a metaphor and none of the achingly suggestive contraries (reason/energy, love/hate, attraction/repulsion, restrainer/restrained) is explicitly gendered" ("Blake and Gender," 147). Perhaps what is most striking about *The Marriage* in the context of sexuality is the frontispiece illustration. In this first plate of the text we notice an embracing couple at the bottom of the page. It is quite clear in this case that it is one male and one female figure. Normally in Blake the females are rather unfeminine with no clear breasts or female shapes, but here we have a naked woman seen from behind with a thin waist and quite broad hips and buttocks. Why does Blake emphasize femininity so strongly here? Does he want to point out the basic male-female binary opposition in this his most clearly dualistic work? Is there a change in his view of woman? Does this change have a sexual foundation? Is this pictorial expression in any way related to his experiences of being sexually tempted, described in the notebook poems discussed above?

Perhaps it is at this time that Blake becomes fully aware of the mechanisms behind the male-female dichotomy. Let us return to the *Notebook* to see if we can find out more. After some insertions including phrases similar to the ones already discussed, we must move on to entry 18 according to Keynes's order, "In a Mirtle Shade," before we find anything as substantial. This poem is close to "My Pretty Rose-tree" in its depiction of a person, presumably male, sick with lust for "Blossoms show'ring all around" (2, E 469). The rose has now turned into a myrtle, but the sense of being chained is the same:

> Why should I be bound to thee
> O my lovely myrtle tree?
> Love, free love, cannot be bound
> To any tree that grows on ground [7–10, Keynes, 169].[2]

This seems to be a common sentiment in Blake at the time and we are to find the idea of "free love" more thoroughly expressed in the lamentations of Oothoon in *Visions of the Daughters of Albion,* also produced in 1793. These years shortly before his first experiment of an epic-scale work in *The Four Zoas,* when he had formed the basic components of his own mythological system, must have been formative for him with influences from many different directions. Not only did he have a Moravian background naturally with him, and a later Swedenborgian inspiration (repudiated or not), but he also took some impression from early women's liberation. Accordingly, it has been stated many times that "free love" is a notion used by Mary Wollstonecraft.

In the introduction to *A Vindication* Miriam Brody claims that "Wollstonecraft's name ... became virtually synonymous with free love and Jacobinism" (Brody, 63). "Free love" is, like revolution and Jacobinism, an easily accessible catchword or cliché, which is unfortunately much too handy for commentators to grab, use and perpetuate in relation to Romantic writers of this tendency. But of what, we must ask, does Wollstonecraft's "free love" consist? Does it refer to the "free" love-relation between Wollstonecraft and her first lover, Gilbert Imlay? Since the couple lived together without marrying and even had a child together there is no doubt that by their contemporaries they were regarded as morally lax and were practically condemned by many people, a reputation boosted by William Godwin's then so scandalous book *Memoirs of the Author of A Vindication of the Rights of Woman.* Or does Wollstonecraft's "free love" merely consist of the widespread circulation of her infamous suggestion of a ménage-a-trois with the object of her hopeless infatuation, Henry Fuseli, and his wife? Certainly, as one of the most familiar episodes from her life, there is little doubt that this image greatly contributes to our conception of Wollstonecraft's free love. However, when reading the *Memoirs* one wonders if Godwin knew about this proposal at all:

> She conceived a personal and ardent affection for him. Mr. Fuseli was a married man, and his wife the acquaintance of Mary. She readily perceived the restrictions which this circumstance seemed

to impose upon her; but she made light of any difficulty that may arise out of them [78].

A little further on Godwin acknowledges Wollstonecraft's great affection for Fuseli: "There is no reason to doubt that, if Mr. Fuseli had been disengaged at the period of their acquaintance, he would have been the man of her choice" (79). Yet again he sees no cause for worry: "As it was, she conceived it both practicable and eligible, to cultivate a distinguishing affection for him, and to foster it by the endearments of personal intercourse and a reciprocation of kindness, without departing in the smallest degree from the rules she prescribed to herself" (79). Hence, there are good reasons to doubt the authenticity of this famous anecdote of Wollstonecraft's "free love." What is further striking is that in a biography which caused a scandal at its publication, Godwin did not even include the most notoriously scandalous episode from her turbulent life.

However, Wollstonecraft was not the only writer of the Romantic period using the term who had far-advanced ideas about free love. It can also be found in the philosophy of her husband William Godwin and, maybe most notably, in the radical opinions of his disciple Percy Bysshe Shelley. In *The Revolt of Islam,* for instance, he sketches a form of sexual utopia, as Claire Tomalin points out: "It involved a sympathetic delineation of a feminist leader and a determined presentation of erotic freedom as part of the revolutionary programme." The poem includes a shocking and incestuous rape, and according to Tomalin it offers "a sexual idyll between hero and heroine in a rural retreat" (58).

Of what, then, does Blake's "free love" consist? Admittedly, there was a period in the early 1790s when Blake seems to have been intrigued by this notion and we can trace such ideas in, for instance, "My Pretty Rosetree." There are several more examples in Blake's *Notebook* at that time of poems, or sketches of poems, with the same theme of forbidden love. Considering his cooperation with Wollstonecraft on her *Original Stories* and her translation from the German *Elements of Morality,* his idea of free love may have been influenced by her supposed suggestion to Blake's good friend Fuseli, and in turn our conception of it may also be. There is another well-known anecdote, of course, that Blake suggested to his wife to bring a handmaiden into their household around this time. However, most notoriously (in)famous is the anecdote that William and Catherine used to play Adam and Eve while reading *Paradise Lost* in their garden at Hercules Buildings in Lambeth. No matter whether they walked around naked in their garden or not, it is deplorable that this episode is one of the first that spring to mind of non–Blakean people when the great poet's name is mentioned. It is quite telling that the popular novelist Tracey Chevalier has had the audacity to build a whole novel, *Burning Bright,* around this anecdote.[3]

Most conspicuously, however, the notion of free love is used in *Visions of the Daughters of Albion* from 1793, which is of course the poem where Blake most evidently applied Wollstonecraftian beliefs, most notably from the *Vindication.* It is here that Oothoon is happy to provide her counterpart Theotormon with other women. It is also specifically this passage that has provided several critics with worthwhile material for their grave misinterpretation and harsh criticism of Blake's view of sexuality. Thus, the notion of free love has been a contributing factor that Blake's sexual politics was for long completely misunderstood. By critics like Anne Mellor, Alicia Ostriker and Brenda Webster he was regarded as a misogynist and sexist.[4] That he was no such thing has been demonstrated in prominent recent studies by, for instance, Helen Bruder and Tristanne Connolly. As Bruder contends in her recent analysis of *Visions:*

> Though problematic, the free love which she [Oothoon] recommends (7.16–22) is unarguably screamed in defiance of greedy masculine assimilation.... This is majestic feminist rhetoric, though dilemmas of course remain ["Blake and Gender Studies," 143].[5]

It is in fact quite the opposite. Much like Wollstonecraft's strong female ideal, in his prophetic poems Blake portrays several powerful female characters taking different kinds of liberties, something which was quite radical in his time. What Wollstonecraft did in her philosophical writing, Blake did in his fictive writing. And just like Wollstonecraft as a person was often condemned and castigated, Blake's women have been similarly misconstrued. Thus, we can draw an interesting and remarkable parallel between real life and fictive characters. In addition, an illuminating comparison can be made between the societies two centuries back and now: a woman who is strong, smart and sexually active always instigates fear and envy — not only in the male sex. To some extent, I suppose, this is a reflection upon female emancipation, then and now: this is how liberated our minds really are.

In 1797, the same year that Mary Wollstonecraft died in childbirth,

William Blake began his first long epic poem, *The Four Zoas*. After a trial period of some five years with several minor prophecies, his radical ideas had now amalgamated into a functional mythological system with characters representing different aspects of the human psyche. It is tempting to suggest that some of Wollstonecraft's energy and urge for an equal society and improved conditions for women went into Blake's visionary work to create a fictitious utopian existence of gender equality in the three major prophecies. If one, as I do, reads Blake's female characters as taking an active part in the poems, some of the comments on Wollstonecraft point to intriguing similarities: "The ideal woman pictured in the *Vindication* is active and intelligent, blending civic and familial responsibilities, freed from drudgery and debasing frugality," writes Miriam Brody, for instance (62).

I will soon return to *Visions*, but first we must move on in the *Notebook*. In poem number 20 we again find an optimistic speaker seeking to fulfill his heartfelt desires, only to be ridiculed by an ignorant society:

> In the morning I went
> As rosy as morn
> To seek for new Joy,
> But I met with scorn [5–8, Keynes, 171].

Perhaps significantly, the next poem is "To Nobodaddy." This Urizenic character is the embodiment of so many negative phenomena in Blake: jealousy, darkness, obscurity, laws and, indeed, ignorance. Most pertinently, the short poem ends with a question directed to womankind: "Or is it because Secresy gains females loud applause?" (9, E 471).

The subsequent poem, the first draft of "The Lilly," has traditionally not been read in a gender context, but if we are to follow the symbolism we have used so far it may well fit the picture. Most significantly, we again encounter the jealous rose that "puts forth a thorn" (1, K 171). In contrast, the innocent "lilly white shall in love delight" (3, K 171). In digesting a poem like this, it would of course be interesting to have a more extensive knowledge of Blake's personal life at that time. Who was the "lilly white" and why did that woman have such profound influence on Blake and his poetry? If we knew the answer to this tough question, a number of vital issues in Blake would be more readily interpreted, not least the gender issue.

If we jump the early draft of "The Nurse's Song" and move on to number 24, in this celebration of youth we find ideas similar to the ones expressed to the contemporaneous *Visions of the Daughters of Albion:*

> Are not the joys of morning sweeter
> Than the joys of night
> And are the vigrous joys of youth
> Ashamed of the light [1–4, E 471].

For one thing, these lines remind us of Blake's comments on masturbation in *Visions:*

> The moment of desire! the moment of desire! The virgin
> That pines for man; shall awaken her wombs to enormous joys
> In the secret shadow of her chamber; the youth shut up from
> The lustful joy. shall forget to generate. & create an amorous image
> In the shadows of his curtains and in the folds of his silent pillow
> [7: 3–7, E 50].

It is indeed significant that Blake goes on to condemn masturbation as an act of secrecy and darkness, promoted by state religion: "Are not these the places of religion? the rewards of continence? / The self enjoyings of self denial? Why dost thou seek religion?" (7: 8–9, E 50). Instead, Blake believes love is nothing to be ashamed of and should be made in the open: "Is it because acts are not lovely, that thou seekest solitude, / Where the horrible darkness is impressed with reflections of desire" (7: 10–11, E 50). This idea has a striking resemblance to the commandments of both the Moravians and Swedenborgians. As noted before, it was imperative for newly wed Moravian couples to make love in front of the elderly of the congregation, while the founding principle for the Swedenborgian Sierra Leone colony was to be marriage with the conjugal duties being regularly performed. Finally, as another echo from the notebook, old Nobodaddy, the "Father of Jealousy" is called upon in the next line.

Also ignoring "How to Know Love from Deceit," which brings up already familiar themes, we turn to entry number 32, "Soft Snow":

> I walked abroad in a snowy day
> I askd the soft snow with me to play
> She playd & she melted in all her prime
> And the winter calld it a dreadful crime [1–4, E 473].

Analyzed along the lines of the present chapter, this poem reads as an unusually open statement of sexual activities carried out. To start with, there seem to be plenty of temptations in a female guise around the speaker of these lines: it is a "snowy day." That this refers to women becomes evident in the next two lines where the "soft snow" is a she. This unknown woman is penetrated in sexual intercourse and apparently quite successfully since she reaches climax in orgasm: "she melted in all her prime." However successful this sexual encounter is, it is nevertheless condemned by a crass society, "winter," which calls "it a dreadful crime." In other words, it is the same old story repeated all over again.

There is no doubt that Blake was prepossessed with these matters, and we find poem 18 repeated, this time as "To my Mirtle." The main ideas are then neatly summed up in "Merlin's Prophecy":

> The harvest shall flourish in wintry Weather
> When two virginities meet together
> The King & the Priest must be tied in a tether
> Before two virgins can meet together [1–4, E 473].

It is however quite problematic to settle how fortunate, or if at all, Blake/the poet was in his lover's pursuit. If we are to use the remarkable sequence of poems between 39 and 43 as evidence, the answer would certainly be negative. In the first, Blake again makes use of an anatomic sexual symbolism, where "the sword" denotes the penis and "the sickle" the vagina:

> The sword sung on the barren heath
> The sickle in the fruitful field
> The sword he sung a song of death
> But could not make the sickle yield [1–4, E 473].

This piece is loaded with sexual frustration and unfulfilled desire; in spite of strong efforts the speaker is not allowed to make love with his fancied object. The next poem follows naturally, indicating the outcome of the two possible alternatives:

> Abstinence sows sand all over
> The ruddy limbs & flaming hair
> But Desire Gratified
> Plants fruits of life & beauty there [1–4, E 473].

Since biographic information tells us that Blake was slightly red-haired and that at times it looked as though his hair was on fire, it is easy to identify the speaker of these lines, and most likely of the whole sequence, with him. Breaking the pattern of quatrain stanzas, in the following piece he blatantly spells out his ideal:

> In a wife I would desire
> What in whores is always found
> The lineaments of gratified desire [1–3, E 473].

We have seen most of this before, of course, but the reference to prostitutes is an unusual one in Blake and again stresses his desperation in this seemingly loveless situation. And most definitely it again points to the problems in Blake's marriage. It is really a dreadfully harsh critique of his faithful wife and we can only wonder how Catherine managed to digest statements like this—if she ever read them, that is. As we know that Blake returned to work with this poem repeatedly in the *Notebook*, it must have been close to his heart. But in the next item the poet appears more uncertain about the right step to take, and whether it is advisable to proceed immediately in the present circumstances:

> If you trap the moment before it's ripe
> The tears of repentance you'll certainly wipe
> But if once you let the ripe moment go
> You can never wipe off the tears of woe [1–4, E 470].

It looks as if it is chiefly a question of judgment: Is the moment now ripe? If it is, there is little doubt about what Blake's panacea is for lovers. This was indicated already in the last two lines in this poem and is even more explicit in the final poem of the sequence, entitled "Eternity":

> He who binds to himself a joy
> Does the winged life destroy
> But he who kisses the joy as it flies
> Lives in eternity's sunrise [1–4, E 470].

This is a well-known maxim that we find repeated several times throughout Blake's oeuvre.

To find the next appropriate example we have to move on quite some bit. When we arrive at entry 53 it seems as if Blake/the speaker has become more and more disappointed, or even resigned:

> The look of love alarms
> Because tis filled with fire
> But the look of soft deceit
> Shall win the lovers hire [1–4, E 474].

Possibly we can deduce from this that Blake had a rival who won the object of his desire over by more or less foul and tricky play. The speaker of the

Notebook poems has just managed to scare the lady off with his open-hearted and impulsive advances. These few lines also remind us of the later poem "Mary" from *The Pickering Manuscript,* with its well-known line "Why was I born with a different face?" (21–2, E 487), in which the speaker with obvious (auto)biographical reference wishes that (s)he was like the rest of the human race. In the above poem the speaker feels just as misplaced and abnormal with his intense feelings of love. We shall return to "Mary" in a short while. In the final specimen dealing with this issue in the *Notebook* we get the reactions of the woman in question as the speaker of the poem:

> An old maid early-eer I knew
> Ought but the love that on me grew
> And now Im coverd oer & oer
> And wish that I had been a Whore
> O I cannot find
> The undaunted courage of a Virgin Mind
> For Early I in love was crost
> Before my flower of lost [1–8, E 474].

Another drastic reference to prostitution, but this time it is a female speaker using this image to indicate that one must not miss out on love's opportunity but, rather, "kiss joy as it flies." If not, you risk ending up as an old maid who has never lost her virginity and experienced real love.

In an additional poem, "A Fairy Skipt upon my Knee," Blake extols the beauty of womankind. Not only does he praise the female form, he finds great cause to celebrate the life of women as a whole:

> Knowest thou not O Fairies Lord
> How much by us Contemnd, Abhorrd
> Whatever hides the Female form
> That cannot bear the Mental storm
> Therefore in Pity still we give
> Our lives to make the Female live
> And what would turn into disease
> We turn to what will joy & please [9–16, E 482].

Surely, the writer of these laudable lines could not have been a misogynist.

As we now approach *Visions of the Daughters of Albion,* one of Blake's key-texts on sexuality, we may find a more substantial use of Moravian and Swedenborgian material. To begin with, the name of the poem's heroine, Oothoon, was probably picked up from the Swedenborgian circles that Blake frequented for a few years. The French concert violinist, conductor, hymn-writer and supporter of the female cause, Francois Barthélemon, who was one of the ninety-five delegates at the 1789 East Cheap conference that Blake socialized with, wrote a poem called "Oithoon" and it is not unlikely that Blake took the name from it.

One of the first things that strikes us when reading *Visions* in this context is the significant use of flower symbolism. The crucial activity of the whole poem is of course Oothoon's plucking of the flower, something which we find explicitly stated already in "The Argument" which stands as a prologue to the poem:

> I plucked Leutha's flower,
> And I rose up from the vale;
> But the terrible thunders tore
> My virgin mantle in twain [5–8, E 45].

Here we find the gist of the poem neatly compressed into eight lines. Innocent at the start of the poem, the speaker Oothoon truly loves Theotormon but unfortunately finds sexual experience elsewhere, which Bromion takes advantage of and rapes her. Sexual jealousy and other complications inevitably quickly ensue.

But the picture is of course more complex than this. There are also, as always with Blake, several possible readings, so we do best to stick with our Swedenborgian/Moravian focus for now. However, I will get back to the poem in the next chapter, focusing on the slavery theme. We may start by asking ourselves about the flower symbolism so significant at the outset of the poem. Where and when did Blake pick that up? It seems to enter roughly at the time of *Visions,* among other poems, since we found it in the *Notebook* too.

Most noteworthy of course are the sexual connotations. The seductive Marygold urges Oothoon to try out the temptations of love she is presented with:

> pluck thou my flower Oothoon the mild
> Another flower shall spring, because the soul of sweet delight
> Can never pass away. she ceasd & closd her golden shrine.
> Then Oothoon pluck'd the flower saying, I pluck thee from thy bed
> Sweet flower. and put thee here to glow between my breasts
> And thus I turn my face to where my whole soul seeks [1: 8–13, E 46].

The flower imagery resulting in Oothoon's sexual initiation has an immediate positive impact at this place of the poem as she in a jubilant mode sets the emotive quest on her true love, Theotormon:

> Over the waves she went in wing'd exulting swift delight;
> And over Theotormon's reign, took her impetuous course [1: 14–15, E 46].

I would further argue that this kind of imagery is in a covert way used to express a Moravian-like glorification of the genital, or erotic, region; here we find the female breasts and "golden shrine," denoting the vagina. But most striking overall about this passage is its positive and elated mood, expressed for instance by the word "delight" being used twice.

In the next passage, very abruptly, Bromion suddenly enters and violently rapes Oothoon. With this truly Blakean twist she is changed from innocent virgin to condemned harlot in an instant's work—at least in Bromion's Urizenic eyes, which serves to introduce the fearful force of jealousy at this early point of the poem: "behold this harlot here on Bromions bed, / And let the jealous dolphins sport around the lovely maid (1: 18–19, E 46). Mission(s) accomplished, and for the remainder of the poem the mood is dramatically altered. The rest mainly consists of the triangular sufferings from the negative repercussions of love of the main characters Oothoon, Bromion and Theotormon. It is also through this critique of a repressive patriarchal system that Blake's great insight and foresight of the negative workings of a gendered society is at its most effective, something which Helen Bruder also points out:

> Blake's description of the hateful sexual compulsions of legally enforced matrimony forges an unbreakable link with feminist discourse which criticism must illuminate further. Similarly important are his revelations about patriarchy's indoctrination of its "accursed" values (7.12–13, 6.7–9); the unsettling of fixed systems of sexual difference through scrutinizing, reversing or re-gendering key stereotypes: virgin, whore, harlot, "hypocrite modesty" (6.16, 6.4–21); and, of course, Oothoon's much vaunted eroticism ["Blake and Gender," 143].

Is the outcome of *Visions* wholly negative then? In contrast to many commentators of the poem, I do not believe so. For instance, the late passage where Oothoon advocates promiscuity has nearly univocally been described by other commentators as a representation of a female character, Oothoon, succumbing to a repressive patriarchal sexual system. To the contrary, I believe it is an expression of the Swedenborgian principle that sexual love is to be shared with several other persons of the other sex. Possibly, this can also relate to the early ideas of the Moravians, at least until the moral outcry and reformation during Sifting time. Oothoon takes unselfish delight in this activity:

> But silken nets and traps of adamant will Oothoon spread,
> And catch for thee girls of mild silver, or of furious gold;
> I'll lie beside thee on a bank & view their wanton play
> In lovely copulation, bliss on bliss, with Thotormon [7: 23–6, E 50].

Oothoon goes on to manifest her innocence and joy by pointing to positive parallels to nature and the animal kingdom and, significantly, she concludes her speech in the poem with the typically Blakean maxim "for every thing that lives is holy!" (8: 10, E 51). Thus, this is her, and Blake's, ideal existence, which will be more emphatically expressed in the long prophetic poems in a more elaborate and complex way. But here at the end of *Visions,* in spite of being holy, the characters and all the embodiments of life are still caught by Bromion's chains of a fallen world.[6]

There is little doubt that *Visions of the Daughters of Albion* is Blake's most developed and mature enunciation of his radical ideas of sex and gender so far. *America,* which is the next poem in rough chronological order, is longer and to a large extent deals with other issues, but at the same time follows the line of development. It is as if Blake goes beyond the superficial level to explore the mechanisms behind a gendered society, as Bruder remarks: "*America,* then, shows Blake's profound awareness that gender operates beyond the confines of individual psychology: a historical process, revolution, is shown to have sexual identity" ("Blake and Gender," 149). Altogether clearly a more political poem, there is a connection to the earlier poem found in the "Preludium," where in a rape-like scene reminiscent of Bromion's rape of Oothoon, the shadowy Daughter of Urthona encounters her newly born son, the fiery boy Orc:

> Silent as despairing love, and strong as jealousy,
> The hairy shoulders rend the links, free are the wrists of fire;
> Round the terrific loins he siez'd the panting struggling womb;
> It joy'd: she put aside her clouds & smiled her first-born smile
> [2: 1–4, E 52].

Thus, Blake's important revolutionary character Orc is born and the poem takes a different direction onwards.

In *Europe: a Prophecy*, from 1793, we find some premature components of a "feminist" Blake. Important new female characters are introduced. Enitharmon appears consistently in *Europe* and Leutha and Oothoon are also mentioned, later to be used in *Milton*. The other female characters have little used names in the Blake oeuvre like "lovely jealous Ocalythron" (8: 7, E 62) and "Ethinthus, queen of waters" (14: 1, E 65), so it is obvious that Blake's mythological world has not yet reached its final stage. This is most clear in the character who is soon to become Vala, here simply labeled "the nameless shadowy female" (1: 1, E 60). Blake's view of the fall and how to share its burden of guilt as equally as possible between male and female also finds one of its first expressions in this poem.

Europe, written and illustrated at approximately the same time, is something of a companion poem to *America*. The former poem, however, lends itself more easily to an analysis in line with gender and sexual issues. Already in the unnumbered introductory plate we notice similarities in symbolism, particularly to *Visions*, and then more significantly to flowers, as the narrator encounters a fairy who dictates the poem to him:

> Wild flowers I gather'd & he shew'd me each eternal flower
> He laugh'd aloud to see them whimper because they were pluck'd.
> They hover'd round me like a cloud of incense [iii: 20–22, E 60].

In the following "Preludium" plates two of the foremost female characters of Blake's long epic prophecies are introduced:

> The nameless shadowy female rose from out the breast of Orc
> Her snaky hair brandishing in the winds of Enitharmon [1: 1–2, E 60].

Maybe significantly both Enitharmon and the Shadowy Female are among the most negative female characters in Blake's poems. Again echoing *Visions*, the Shadowy Female questions her mother Enitharmon: "Ah! I am drown'd in shady woe and visionary joy. / And who shall bind the infinite with an eternal band?" (2: 12–13, E 61). The mood conveyed here, clearly of a fallen world, reminds us of the chilled atmosphere of "The Night of Enitharmon's Joy," also known as "Hecate," one of Blake's most famous large watercolor paintings from this period. And not surprisingly, an allusion to this painting is what we find in plate 5, one of the most controversial in Blake's poetry from a gender political perspective:

> Now comes the night of Enitharmon's joy!
> Who shall I call? Who shall I send

> That Woman, lovely Woman, may have dominion?
> Arise, O Rintrah, thee I call! & Palamabron, thee
> Go! Tell the Human race that Woman's love is Sin
> That an Eternal life awaits the worms of sixty winters
> In an allegorical abode where existence has never come.
> Forbid all Joy & from her childhood shall the little female
> Spread nets in every secret path [5: 1–9, E 62].

Here once again it should be underscored that Blake's art and poetry must be read and interpreted in its entirety, with a holistic view. Such an analysis is particularly important with a much debated passage like plate 5 of *Europe*. Read in the light of the complex mythological system that Blake was soon to develop into completion in the major epics, but which could already be discerned here to a large extent, the outcome of this plate is not that negative. It is not, as nearly all commentators have believed, a castigation of woman as a human being. *Europe* takes place entirely on a fallen level, and in that world Enitharmon is the dominant female character who attempts to govern her fellow sisters by commanding them to proclaim the sinfulness of female love. She may dominate this poem, but as Blake becomes clearer about his basic ideas by a considerable extension of his mythological scope, more positive women characters see the light of day to counterbalance the negativity of Enitharmon and the Shadowy Female. But here it seems that Blake uses Enitharmon to state a negative example. Rather than a castigation, the passage is a warning.

Further evidence of the negativity of *Europe* is the eighteen-hundred-years-long sleep of Enitharmon, with woman again used as an antithesis: "Eighteen hundred years, a female dream" (9: 5, E 63). However, at the end of the poem there are signs that Enitharmon awakens from her sleep. For one thing, there are several apocalyptic harbingers like trumpets, vineyards, golden chariots, and the end of time appears to be imminent: "That nature felt thro all her pores the enormous revelry / Till morning opened the eastern gate" (14: 34–5, E 66). But also, a couple of characters that will gain prominence in the later epics are introduced here: Leutha, who is to assume the role of leading female negation in *Milton*, is, remarkably, launched as a more positive character, the "Soft soul of flowers" (14: 11, E 65). Most significantly, though, Oothoon enters, providing an even stronger reverberation from *Visions*. Enitharmon, with Oothoon's promulgation of the innocence of "free love" fresh in mind, accuses her of betraying woman's supreme position to man: "Why wilt thou give up woman's secrecy, my melancholy child?" (14: 22, E 66).

When we now move on to what are commonly known as Blake's Urizen books, there is again less emphasis on sexual issues. There are a few significant inclusions, however. In the first of these books, *The Song of Los,* there is not a lot to mention. This work is divided into two sections, "Africa" and "Asia," thus announcing a discourse more concerned with political and postcolonial matters. As we realize from the subheadings, it was somehow also intended to complement *Europe* and *America.* One passage, though, refers back to *Visions* by recalling Oothoon and by calling attention to the incident of the binding of Orc with the chain of jealously, more fully described elsewhere.[7] In general, mankind is in a bad state: "The human race began to wither, for the healthy built / secluded places, fearing the joys of Love" (3: 25–6, E 67). As Blake next makes clear, in his view this is accomplished through the negative institutions of "churches, Hospitals, Castles, Palaces" which "catch the joys of Eternity" (4: 1–2, E 67).

The next poem, *The Book of Ahania,* is more engaged with gender ideas. Early on we even get a brief glimpse at the male-female division in the creation of man, so crucial to Blake:

> Urizen dividing
> Dire shriekd his invisible Lust
> Deep groand Urizen! Stretching his awful hand
> Ahania (so name his parted soul)
> He seizd on his mountain of Jealousy.
>
> He groand anguishd & calld her Sin
> Kissing her and weeping over her
> Then hid her in darkness, in silence
> Jealous, tho' she was invisible [2: 29–37, E 84].

The gender division is maintained throughout the poem and the main protagonist Ahania calls out in desperation for her lost consort:

> To awake bright Urizen, my king
> To arise to the mountain sport
> To the bliss of eternal valleys
>
> To awake my king in the morn
> To embrace Ahania's joy
> On the bredth of his open bosom? [5: 7–12, E 89].

This passage surely has a sexual connotation, with "mountain sport" and "arise" alluding to the male genitals and "eternal valleys" to the female. We have this more or less confirmed a bit further on, as Blake echoes the beautiful and metaphorically loaded language of the Song of Solomon:

> My ripe figs and rich pomegranates
> In infant joy at thy feet
> O Urizen sported and sang
>
> Then with thy lap full of seed
> With thy hand full of generous fire
> Walked forth from the clouds of morning
> On the virgins of springing joy
> On the human soul to cast
> The seed of eternal science [5: 26–34, E 89].

Urizen performs his male activities of pleasure, sporting and singing, as he makes love to Ahania. He clearly fulfils his desire at this point through ejaculation since Ahania has her "lap full of seed."

The Book of Los, which follows, also harks back to happier pre-lapsarian times:

> O Times remote!
> When Love & Joy were adoration
> And none impure were deemd
> Not Eyeless Covet
> Nor Thin-lipd envy
> Nor Bristled Wrath
> Nor Curled Wantonness [3: 7–13, E 90].

But in the creation and fall, which Blake considered to have taken place simultaneously, this innocent love and joy were lost and all these virtues were turned into negations:

> But Covet was poured full
> Envy fed with fat of lambs
> Wrath with lion's gore
> Wantonness lulld to sleep
> With the virgin's lute
> Or sated with her love [3: 14–19, E 90].

Even the eternally fighting and laboring poet-artist Los falls endlessly and the light is lost to immense darkness.

Blake's Sexuality

As is well known, the poems that Blake was to create next, in the period of some twenty years after 1795, are not only long and epically structured but also immensely complex. To most readers they are complicated and often present an insurmountable challenge. However, by using Blake's fully developed mythological system as an interpretative key the task becomes considerably less daunting. Already in *The Four Zoas*, begun in the years right after the shorter Lambeth poems, 1795–97, Blake had settled for a successful poetic structure which he was to keep in the later *Milton* and *Jerusalem*. Of course, these two epics are much more fully drawn artistic creations, and in *The Four Zoas* we frequently encounter somewhat sketchy, bewildering, hard-to-interpret and not always logical passages. There may after all have been good reasons for Blake choosing not to engrave this poem, only the other two.

Quite naturally, there is a lot of rewarding material in the three poems for our discussion of sex and gender. They are particularly rewarding as a delineation of the eternal battle of the sexes in a fallen world, which in Blake's view was an inevitable outcome of the male-female division in the fall. They are also fruitful as a comment on the growing concern for a better society in terms of gender equality. However, my main concern here is not a socially and politically inclined lengthy discussion; rather, I will provide some background of the basic structure and ideas of the poems in relation to issues of sexuality. Naturally, I will also relate them to Moravian and Swedenborgian characteristics.[8]

Blake's what most frequently misunderstood ideas are probably his ideas of sex, love, relations and the female. As all Blakeans know, his female characters have generally been interpreted negatively. I would suggest, rather (even though an individual character may be negative), that in the long run ALL Blake's women characters in the three epics must be read positively. Through their actions they all contribute fundamentally to the positive outcomes of the poems. In *The Four Zoas*, for instance, Vala and Enitharmon often have negative implications, but for the final resurrection of mankind the activity of these two characters is just as important as that of the traditionally more positively read Ahania and Enion. In the ninth night Vala, in the passage commonly known as "Vala's Garden," visualizes a bucolic, pleasant existence in a dream-like mood. This is one of the harbingers of the apocalypse at the finish of the poem. Another similar episode is when Enitharmon together with her corresponding zoa Los/Urthona take down Christ from the cross at the end of the eighth night. Enitharmon is also the first emanation to be reconciled with her zoa at the close of the poem.

In the three epic prophecies *The Four Zoas*, *Milton* and *Jerusalem* Blake finally found a way to portray his female characters as uncommonly active in gender relations. Like Wollstonecraft, Blake emphasized the inner values of the human mind and in these three long poems he significantly internalized the impulse of erotic desire to ultimately belong to his utopian world of Eden where the aim was an equal, even genderless, society. However, he did not abandon the sexual impulse for this ideal existence; rather, like Wollstonecraft, he directed it heavenward through his fantasizing mind. Like Swedenborg, Blake believed that after death we continue the life we were leading here on earth in another form of existence. For both Blake and Wollstonecraft, and then of course particularly for Blake, the imagination was the supreme faculty. In Wollstonecraft's *Mary, or, the Wrongs of Woman* the main protagonist "was hastening towards that world where there is neither marrying, nor giving in marriage" (92). Significantly, Blake also uses this Biblical passage from Matthew in *Jerusalem* where Albion says to Vala: "In Eternity they neither marry nor are given in marriage" (34: 15, E 176).[9]

The representation of sexuality in Blake's utopia is one of the most debated issues and probably the most difficult to clearly comprehend. Since he posits something of an androgynous ideal it is tempting to believe that he completely discards sexuality on this level, which is what most commentators do. I cannot agree with this view. Naturally, we cannot say either with any conviction; as little as we can prove that there is no sex in Eden, it is impossible to establish that sexuality exists at that level. It was all in Blake's imagination and the poems do not provide us with any clear evidence either way.

However, since the road to Eden, according to Blake, goes via the union of the male and the female, both in body and in mind, what is most logical is that he visualized some sort of sexuality to be kept. One thing that we can be sure of is that the negative implications of sex, such as erotic desire and jealousy, were not to remain. Those, as we know, are the main obstacles of our fallen world that prevent us from an existence in peace and happiness, and this impulse, instead of generating love, leads to its negation — war and hunger for power. Then, if we try to reason logically again, in the utopia Blake envisions the erotic impulse takes the opposite positive direction and becomes the generator of love.

Therefore, it is likely that the male-female union, or rather re-union (since the sexes according to Blake were divided in the fall and have to undergo a constant battle in this world), was to be one of equality and togetherness, in intellectual community. Here it is considerably easier for the literary critic since there is blatant textual evidence in the three epics. In these poems the battle of the sexes is described in various ways. The sexual warfare rages on throughout the poems: in *The Four Zoas* with the zoas seeking to re-unite in harmony with their counterpart emanations; in *Milton* with Ololon's search for her consort in the mundane world; in *Jerusalem* with the eponymous character's almost desperate attempts to re-awaken Albion in order to save mankind. In two of them we have happy endings: *The Four Zoas* and *Jerusalem* conclude with man and woman re-united in harmonious togetherness, while *Milton* finishes on the verge of apocalypse but in harmony created by the insertion in the last few plates of several utopian portent symbols like swallows and thyme. The most remarkable aspect of the magnificent endings of Blake's epics are the mis-interpretations, or perhaps neglect, from so many critics and readers of Blake throughout the years. True enough, these are extremely difficult poems, but even so it is striking that Blake's crucial love message has been so completely missed by otherwise sensible and competent commentators.

When Blake begins *The Four Zoas* he appears to have a more or less finished idea of what is by now a fully developed mythological system. At least this could be said about his characters, which are now logically organized into four male zoas and four emanations. Once one has grasped this structure, there is little doubt which emanation belongs to which zoa. On the other hand, the plot and action of this poem is by far not as clear-cut as the characters, and Blake still had much work to do to refine this aspect for the following two poems. *The Four Zoas* is after all an unfinished poem, which often leaves the reader with a chaotic impression, so even though Blake had his ideas clear to himself there was still a lot to be asked of their execution and presentation.

Of course, *The Four Zoas* is an extremely important poem in the Blake corpus. Nearly all the major characters are now in place, apart from a few more that will be introduced in *Milton* and *Jerusalem*. It is true that most of them have taken part of one or several in the minor prophecies, but it is only now that they are all to be found in one poem. It is something of the defining moment for these characters, and the most fundamental achievement is the positioning of the four zoas—Los, Urizen, Tharmas, Luvah—and coupling them with their four emanations: Enitharmon, Ahania, Enion and Vala. The last of these, of course, was the eponymous "heroine" of the first draft of the poem that Blake conceived.

As we now have these central characters, evenly divided into male and female, the stage is set for the eternal battle of the sexes in a fallen world—a play in nine acts, or nights, as Blake labeled them, taking the cue from Young's *Night Thoughts,* which Blake illustrated at the time and which he used to write many of the pages in the *Zoas* manuscript on. We are already thrown into the irrevocably fallen condition of this existence on the first page, as Tharmas announces:

> Lost! Lost! Lost! Are my Emanations! Enion, O Enion,
> We are become a Victim to the living. We hide in secret.
> I have hidden Jerusalem in silent Contrition, O Pity Me [1: 25–7, E 301].

Clearly, the classical and most negative components, to Blake at least, of a fallen world—sexual desire and jealousy—have already come into play here. And the state of things is going to stay pretty much like this for the remainder of the poem.

It is a tale of continual struggle and of fear and terror, as Enion points out early on:

> Thy fear has made me tremble, thy terrors have surrounded me.
> All Love is lost: Terror succeeds & hatred instead of Love
> And stern demands of Right & Duty instead of Liberty [1: 35–7, E 301].

Although the chaotic and sometimes incoherent structure of the poem is an aesthetic flaw, at the same time it lends support to the overall message that what we live in is a fallen world and that there is endless affliction and suffering for mankind to go through before we can reach an improved existence. It is only by labor and hardship that we can overcome our troubles and redeem the fall—a long and winding road which Blake tries symbolically to show us in *The Four Zoas.*

Therefore, the most important contribution of the poem, besides the original division into zoas and emanations, is its apocalyptic and utopian ending. In Night nine, towards the conclusion of the poem, the actions of the characters suddenly become more positive and Blake introduces a whole number of apocalyptic images. Los and Enitharmon start building the utopian city of Jerusalem and Jesus is resurrected from his tomb. Then Los

> Siez'd the Sun; His left hand, like dark roots, cover'd the Moon
> And tore them down, cracking the heavens from immense to immense.
> Then fell the fires of Eternity with loud & shrill
> Sound of Loud Trumpet thundering along from heaven to heaven
> A mighty sound articulate [9: 8–12, E 386].

As is obvious, Blake appropriates traditional apocalyptic images from the Bible. But not only does he make use of them — he also refines them. It is difficult to think of a more accomplished transmitter of the apocalypse than Blake. In this, *The Four Zoas* is the work of a true bard.

What is most unique, then, is the very conclusion with each male zoa finding his counterpart emanation for reunion in the apocalypse. After the apocalyptic workings in Night nine, all four couples have by now redeemed themselves and are ready to enter the post-apocalyptic utopian after-world. In this wonderful existence every one and every thing is equal and the differences between the sexes are erased; gender equality is accomplished. A completely new form of life is announced, hitherto unknown to humankind:

> How is it we have walk'd thro' fires & yet are not consum'd?
> How is it that all things are chang'd, even as in ancient times?
> [9: 844–45, E 407].

The last portion of *The Four Zoas* may at first sight seem like a perfectly concluded poem. Apparently this was not the case since Blake, much with the same basic preconceptions, carried on to create *Milton* and *Jerusalem*. That it is not absolutely perfect becomes clear if we read the very last bit of the *Zoas* really carefully. It is then obvious that not all four couples have reached the highest level of togetherness after going through the apocalypse. It is only explicitly stated that Los/Urthona and Enitharmon achieve the full harmony of the last stage, while the other three couples have not yet come fully through. Los and Enitharmon may be the key couple of the poem, but even so it is something of a pyrrhic victory. Hence, the poetic battle must rage on.

What is superficially most conspicuous with Blake's next epic, *Milton*, compared to *The Four Zoas* is that it is confidently organized in two Books with a total of fifty plates, if we are to take the elaborate 1815 copy as the final version.[10] Even though we know that Blake probably intended it to be much longer, consisting of twelve Books (which can clearly be seen on the title page of this copy), he seems at some point in the process to have arrived at the appropriate decision to keep the length down and aim for the structure of the poem as we now know it. It is most likely, of course, that when he began *Jerusalem* before having a definite finished version of *Milton*, some of the twelve-book material went into that poem instead.

Whatever the order of creation was and no matter which poem the material was intended for, it is obvious that Blake at that time had arrived at a form and method that well-suited his means and aims. This is further underscored by the indisputable fact that he illustrated *Milton* with his most beautiful designs so far. Bearing in mind the minutely detailed and necessarily slow-going creative process of his illuminated writing technique, it is not surprising that the final product stands out in a way which was not possible for an unillustrated and unwieldy poem like *The Four Zoas*. When Blake had engraved a word on the copperplate there was little or no chance for him to change it.[11] So while the *Zoas* remains a manuscript poem, with *Milton* we are presented with an accomplished work of art.

While it is often difficult to make out whether *The Four Zoas* is a poem promoting equality, there is little doubt that *Milton* is almost symmetrically divided between a male "hero" and a female "heroine." Book one is devoted to Milton and the story of his descent to the earthly existence and book two deals with his counterpart Ololon's search for him. Hence, even structurally, *Milton* is a poem of gender equality. This is further corroborated as we find out that Ololon is one of Blake's strongest female characters, who is more than able to counterbalance the activity of her consort.

However, the subject matter of *Milton* is in some ways more complex than the *Zoas*. Not only is Milton sent down to earth to rectify his errors with his female relations, he is also supposed to correct what he did wrong in his poetry. This is a possible reason why there is no clear focus on gender reunion at the end of the poem. In spite of its overall progression and its improved symbolism, *Milton* is not a fully apocalyptic poem and none of its characters reach the highest utopian level. It is a development to focus on only one male and one female character, instead of the overly complex structure of four zoas and four emanations, but since Milton and Ololon never achieve togetherness the conclusion of the poem is in that sense an anti-climax. A very beautiful anti-climax, however, with a great atmosphere of harmony among all the creatures and creations participating in this apocalyptic onset. They are all now prepared for the next step of the apocalypse.

The next apocalyptic step is *Jerusalem*. As should be fully clear by now, this is Blake's most accomplished and refined artistic expression which of course is also one of the great masterpieces of British art and literature. It is his final and prophetic word about the crucial issues dealt with in the two preceding epics: religion, sexuality, gender, apocalypse, utopia.

In comparison with the two preceding poems, *Jerusalem* is a much richer poem, saturated from completion. Thus, it deals with considerably more issues than the other two do. On the other hand, it can be claimed that sexuality and gender politics are still its foundational topics. The other issues emerge and revolve around these two issues. Significantly, since it appears that Blake now returns to more obvious Christian themes, he reverts to the Moravian worship of the genitals by creating new symbols like Cathedron (the womb) and Luban (the vagina), both making up the entrance to his holy utopian city, Golgonooza.

Some of the characters from *The Four Zoas* are back in *Jerusalem*, most notably the two main protagonists Los and Enitharmon. These two have a key function in bringing on the apocalypse, but also serve as emblems of the increased gender interactivity. *Jerusalem*, however, belongs to the eponymous female character and her counterpart, the eternal man Albion. The two characters function as metonymical representations of the female and male portions of mankind, respectively. As Jerusalem at long last succeeds in awakening Albion and they are caught up in the ongoing apocalypse, so are all mankind and consequently all earthly organisms too. There is no doubt that, like in *Milton*, the simplified structure with two representational characters is more successful and at the conclusion of *Jerusalem* we can be certain that everyone and everything has reached the highest level of Blake's uniquely visualized utopian existence: "And I heard the Name of their Emanations: they are named Jerusalem" (99: 5, E 259).

When giving a continuous and complete account of Blake's poetry, it is natural that the three major prophecies—*The Four Zoas, Milton*, and *Jerusalem*—should follow logically from the minor prophecies.[12] However, this presents us with a slight problem since it leaves out the late *Notebook* poems, most notably the significant ones from *The Pickering Manuscript*. According to G. E. Bentley, these poems were probably composed between 1800 and 1804, years during which Blake mostly resided at Felpham on the English south coast under the patronage of the gentleman poet William Hayley. Bentley puts the date of transcribing them as fair copies to sometime between 1805 and 1807, after the publication in 1805 of Hayley's *Ballads*, the leaves of which Blake used as writing paper.[13] In any circumstances, the Pickering poems should be chronologically placed after *The Four Zoas* but before or in-between *Milton* and *Jerusalem*, depending on what dates we affix to these two epics.[14]

This small collection of ten fair copy poems gives the overall impression of being of some special importance to Blake.[15] After all, he wrote them down in his finest handwriting, which indicates that he must have had some further intention with them. Why, then, did he leave them as they now are? One reason, perhaps, could be that he had at this time given up the idea of adding more short poems to his catalogue of illuminated writing, mainly consisting of the *Songs*, now that he had dedicated himself to creating epic prophetic poems.

Interestingly, a few of the Pickering poems are also to be found in rougher, tentative drafts in Blake's *Notebook* from 1800–03. Bearing in mind the more or less contemporaneous dates of the two manuscripts,[16] it may be rewarding to discuss both sets of poems to some extent since the main themes are similar throughout. As a natural introduction to *The Pickering Manuscript* I will therefore start by some brief comments about a couple of the *Notebook* poems.

This part of Blake's *Notebook* (according to Keynes, written between 1800 and 1803) begins with a most haunting lyric, "My Spectre Around Me Night & Day." Depending on what we prefer to read into it and into what context we put it, it is clear that on one level it is a frightening account of severe problems in Blake's married life. "My Spectre" is a down-to-earth, literal expression of the same negative and disastrous mechanisms that Blake symbolically depicts in the three epics. Significantly, it is around this time that Blake begins the sometimes autobiographical *Milton*, using the earlier poet as a vehicle to come to terms with his own domestic problems. It appears, then, that the Felpham years were the most problematic in the marriage of William and Catherine.

This *Notebook* poem also introduces the difficult notion of the psychological entity of the "spectre," a concept that Blake had already used in *The Four Zoas*. The spectre is the negation of man, or of the "zoa" which denotes something of our bad conscience that keeps us at bay by pinpointing and bringing all our bad qualities to the surface, an idea later developed by Nietzsche into the "Übermensch" and by Freud into the "id." This is obvious in Blake's text, as the spectre continuously hovers over the speaker:

> My Spectre around me night & day
> Like a Wild beast guards my way.
> My Emanation far within
> Weeps incessantly for my Sin.
> Thy weeping thou shall ne'er give o'er
> I sin against thee more & more
> And never will from sin be free
> Till she forgives & comes to me.
> Thou hast parted from my side:
> Once thou wast a virgin bride.
> Never shalt thou a true love find:
> My Spectre follows thee from Behind [1–12, E 475–76].

The speaker is clearly quite remorseful and suffers sheer hell from his spectre's harsh castigations. He needs his wife's forgiveness to set him free from the inner pain. The problems were apparently increasing over time and the breach between husband and wife now seems most definite. Notably, Blake makes use of other vital concepts from the prophetic books: the female "Emanation" and the need of forgiveness as a redemptive force, which was to become a major idea in *Jerusalem*. It is also obvious that, as in *The Four Zoas*, these terrible tribulations take place on a mental plane within the psyche of the speaker.

It is a serious problem and "A Fathomless & boundless deep / There we wander, there we weep" is predicted for the two protagonists (15–16, E 476). In similarity with *The Four Zoas*, where the emanations are hidden and lost at the onset of the poem, the objects of the speaker's love are driven away in jealousy: "Secret trembling night & day / Driving all my Loves away" (19–20, E 476). That jealousy here is also the driving negative force becomes even clearer as the poem unfolds:

> Dost thou not in Pride & scorn
> Fill with tempests all my morn
> And with jealousies & fears
> Fill my pleasant nights with tears? [13–16, E 476].

Everything is now put to the test with disastrous consequences:

> Seven of my sweet loves thy knife
> Has bereaved of their life.
> Their marble tombs I built with tears
> And with cold shuddering fears.
>
> Seven more loves weep night & day
> Round the tombs where my loves lay
> And seven more loves attend each night
> Around my couch with torches bright [17–24, E 476].

Metaphorically speaking (we must hope), the speaker has devastated quite a number of existences through his amoral actions, "bereaved ... their life." By twisting his "knife" the speaker has caused chronic harm to his victims. He just does not seem to get enough of this perverted pleasure.

"My Spectre" offers something of a mixture of major Blakean ideas, and in the next stanza there are hints of "free love" and forgiveness of sins as the overabundance continues:

> And seven more Loves in my bed
> Crown with wine my mournful head
> Pitying & forgiving all
> Thy transgressions, great & small [25–8, E 476].

This is only one of many remarkable incidents of unconditional and all-embracing forgiveness in Blake's poetry. The central Christian and Moravian notion of forgiveness is a crucial component in Blake's later poetry — particularly in *Jerusalem*. In "My Spectre" the speaker seems to find resolution through this in a positive ending of the poem:

> Let us agree to give up Love
> And root up the infernal grove;
> Then shall we return & see
> The worlds of happy Eternity.
>
> & Throughout all Eternity
> I forgive you, you forgive me [49–54, E 477].

But forgiveness comes with a costly price: love is to be abandoned in eternity. With sexual love implied here, it is evident that although "My Spectre" is certainly an important poem in Blake's philosophical development, his vision is not complete at this stage. To reach that exquisite level two more epic prophecies had to be created.

The focus on troublesome marriage conditions continues in a couple of more instances in the first part of the *Notebook*. In the next brief stanza Blake again takes a swing at sexual love:

> When a Man has Married a Wife
> he finds out whether
> Her knees & elbows are only
> glued together [E 516].

In this frequently personal set of poems we must sometimes, as in this short piece, ask ourselves to what extent Blake is private and to what extent he is open. Does he perhaps speak in more general terms? This poem would certainly appear suitable for those who believe that Blake's marriage was unconsummated. However unlikely I find a platonic relation between William and Catherine, I shall leave this query unanswered.

Most outspoken, however, is this loose couplet: "Terror in the house does roar / But Pity stands before the door" (E 478). With this as one of several pieces of evidence I believe we can now safely establish that the Blakes had serious problems in their marriage for some time, presumably during the Felpham years and shortly after. Together with "My Spectre" and *Milton*, this stinging couplet provides strong autobiographical confirmation of this.

Further proof is offered by the first draft of "The Golden Net,"[17] which was to be included in *The Pickering Manuscript*, and it is to these poems I now turn. "The Golden Net" is the second poem of this manuscript. It is preceded by the relatively bland "The Smile," which, however, does point ahead to major themes in *The Pickering Manuscript*, such as the deceitful and hateful intolerant society we encounter in "Mary" and "William Bond." "The Golden Net" continues the comments on the negations of love. Most likely Blake has the lamentable state of his own marriage in mind since he introduces the golden net as a new symbol representing the net of marriage and its trappings. And this marriage is not in a good state with three virgins, representing fire, iron wire, tears and sighs respectively, enticing the young man of the poem by "[d]azzling bright before [his] eyes" (8, E 483). Through these virgins the man becomes aware of the golden net:

> They bore a Net of Golden twine
> To hang upon the branches fine.
> Pitying I wept to see the woe
> That Love & Beauty undergo

> To be consum'd in burning Fires
> And in ungratified desires
> And in tears cloth'd Night & day
> Melted all my Soul away [9–16, E 483].

The workings of the virgins are conspicuous here in tears and fires, as are also echoes from "My Spectre Around Me Night & Day." Moreover, it appears to be the opposite of the earlier *Notebook* entry number 59 "Several Questions Answered," with its emphasis on "[t]he lineaments of Gratified Desire" (E 474–75).[18] It seems there is no solution to Blake's matrimonial dilemma, and at the end of the poem we find the young man still caught up in the net having made no progress with the three virgins:

> Underneath the Net I stray
> Now intreating Burning Fire
> Now intreating Iron Wire
> Now intreating Tears & Sighs
> O when will the morning rise? [22–6, E 483].

But, of course, how can he make any progress with the Golden Net of marriage hovering over him like a Damocles sword?

"The Mental Traveller," which is the third Pickering poem, may be the most challenging of Blake's poems, disregarding the minor and major prophecies. However, as we shall see as we go along, some of its intricate symbolism becomes more or less self-explanatory. The speaker/traveller announces in the first stanza that we are about to encounter "dreadful things" (3, E 483). This is definitely the case, even though it is not always easy to make out what is what in the often labyrinthine—significantly one of the self-explanatory terms used later on—structure of the poem. We set off on our journey in the joy of innocence: "For there the Babe is born in joy" (5, E 483). This is soon changed and the mood of the poem is established in a most fearful image:

> And if the Babe is born a Boy
> He's given to a Woman Old
> Who nails him down upon a rock
> Catches his shrieks in cups of gold.
>
> She binds iron thorns around his head
> She pierces both his hands and feet
> She cuts his heart out at his side
> To make it feel both cold & heat [9–16, E 484].

A boy-child chained on a rock must certainly be one of Blake's favorite images and, as we have seen, he used it in several places. In most cases the chained boy is Orc, the energetic revolutionary spirit. This frightening passage also has obvious overtones of the crucifixion of Christ, again with a Moravian inclination, emphasizing the piercing of the hands and feet. The picture becomes even more complicated in the next two stanzas:

> Her fingers number every Nerve
> Just as a Miser counts his gold;
> She lives upon his shrieks & cries
> And she grows young as he grows old.
>
> Till he becomes a bleeding youth
> And she becomes a Virgin bright;
> Then he rends up his Manacles
> And binds her down for his delight [17–24, E 484].

This passage further manifests the Moravian influence of this poem, with its emphasis of blood, reminiscent of the Moravians' fixation on the blood of Christ's side-wound. Noteworthy here is also the somewhat unexpected but intriguing metamorphosis of age. Ageing is the most effective image of "The Mental Traveller," but at the same time it is the most difficult to interpret. We can be sure, though, that it affects both sexes equally, since we get the same scenario when next a baby girl is born. Most fittingly the now aged and poor wandering man finds the young maiden:

> And to allay his freezing Age
> The Poor Man takes her in his arms;
> The Cottage fades before his sight
> The Garden & its lovely Charms.
>
> The Guests are scatter'd thro' the land
> For the Eye altering alters all;
> The Senses roll themselves in fear
> And the flat Earth becomes a Ball [57–64, E 485].

This amazing and uncanny passage makes poems like Coleridge's "The Ancient Mariner" and "Christabel," and Keats's "La Belle Dame Sans Merci" and "Lamia" come to mind, and if any poem in the Blake corpus can be said to be Gothic "The Mental Traveller" is the one. Like the aforementioned poems, there is a spellbinding atmosphere about "The Mental Traveller," a transfixion by the piercing stare of the eye, which makes it both compelling and demanding.[19] Furthermore, it is something of a symbiotic relation as the old woman feeds upon the young man and the two change places, as it were. In another Christ-like image the man encounters the same fate as the old woman:

> The honey of her Infant lips
> The bread & wine of her sweet smile
> The wild game of her roving Eye
> Does him to Infancy beguile;
>
> For as he eats & drinks he grows
> Younger & younger every day;
> And on the desert wild they both
> Wander in terror & dismay [69–76, E 485].

Keats's poems were of course written later than "The Mental Traveller" and "Christabel" was first published in 1816, but I would like to suggest that it was quite likely that Blake had read and been inspired by "The Ancient Mariner," published only a few years earlier in the *Lyrical Ballads*. Blake's poem moves full cycle as it concludes:

> Like the wild Stag she flees away
> Her fear plants many a thicket wild;
> While he pursues her night & day
> By various arts of Love beguil'd
>
> By various arts of Love & Hate
> Till the wild desert planted o'er
> With Labyrinths of wayward Love
> Where roams the Lion, Wolf & Boar
>
> Till he becomes a wayward Babe
> And she a weeping Woman Old.
> Then many a Lover wanders here;
> The Sun & Stars are nearer roll'd [77–88, E 485–86].

The poem comes full circle and the original positions are regained, with the man a young baby again and the woman being of old age. This may well be as close as we get to an explication of this notoriously baffling poem: mankind is forever caught up in the labyrinths of wayward love.

"The Mental Traveller" might be the most intriguing and difficult of the Pickering poems, but the most well-known and most frequently cited poem is the slightly longer "Auguries of Innocence." This compilation of wise and acerbic aphorisms, incorporating a vast array of somehow significant animals, includes one of Blake's most famous images, the grain of sand:

>   To see a World in a Grain of Sand
>   And a Heaven in a Wild Flower
>   Hold Infinity in the palm of your hand
>   And Eternity in an hour [1–4, E 490].

Since "Auguries" clearly differs in structure from the other Pickering poems in its rather fragmented build-up and its many scattered issues, it is not my ambition here to give a thorough analysis of it. It does not seem to be of the same overall subject matter, love, as the other poems in *The Pickering Manuscript*. However, the general impression yielded by the poem rhymes well both with the ecstatic but at the same time serene spirit of the Moravians, and in its all-embracing message with one of the main cornerstones of *Jerusalem*.

Possibly the best example of Moravian influence in Blake's poetry is the poem preceding "Auguries," namely "The Grey Monk." Marsha Keith Schuchard's book *Why Mrs Blake Cried* has put Moravianism on the Blake map in a popular, and sometimes at best scholarly, way. Boasting her own and Keri Davies's groundbreaking research and discoveries of the birthplace and Moravian background of Blake's mother, it has given scholars a new impetus for work in hitherto unknown and exciting directions. As much as we may now see Blake's most canonical poetry with new eyes, his Moravian family environment highlights previously obscure and neglected poems.

"The Grey Monk" is an excellent example of such a poem. All things considered, the poems in *The Pickering Manuscript* present several intriguing subjects executed in a well developed and refined style in what look like finished products in fair hand intended for publication, either in a conventional way or in Blake's own illuminated method with complementary illustrations. Since it is clear that the Pickering poems are at an advanced stage of completion, and given their serious subject-matter, we can logically surmise that Blake regarded "The Grey Monk" also as a poem of some importance. Particularly as it is squeezed in-between two of the heavyweights of the collection, "The Crystal Cabinet" with its shrewd and unreserved sexual symbolism and the long and winding, philosophical "Auguries of Innocence."

The challenging ideas of "The Grey Monk" hark back to the extremely controversial period in Moravian history called Sifting Time. The adventurous and provocative period under Zinzendorf with its attempts in sexual, spiritual and racial liberation was both the most creative and disputed time in the history of the Moravians. The Sifting Time led to an uproar among the more conservative members of the church and the period became buried in their archives, not to be brought into the open for centuries. According to Moravian historians, Sifting Time was a period of excess—often sexual—which was centered round the obsessed fascination with the wounds and blood of Christ:

> The Sifting Period was a distortion of a basically sound emphasis upon the atoning death of Christ. Its outward manifestation was a morbid concentration and wordplay upon the blood and wounds of the crucified Christ and a simulated irresponsibility of behaviour supposed to be a demonstration of childlike faith [Weinlick, 198].

It appears that Blake knew about this period with its emphasis on the wounds and blood of Christ and was somehow fascinated by it. It is this idea that we find expressed in the extraordinary "The Grey Monk." The full poem reads:

> I die I die the Mother said
> My Children die for the lack of Bread
> What more has the merciless Tyrant said
> The Monk sat down on the Stony Bed
> The blood red ran from the Grey Monks side
> His hands & feet were wounded wide
> His Body bent his arms & knees
> Like to the roots of ancient trees
> His eye was dry no tear could flow
> A hollow groan first spoke his woe
> He trembled & shudderd upon the Bed
> At length with a feeble cry he said
> When God commanded this hand to write
> In the studious hours of deep midnight
> He told me the writing I wrote should prove
> The Bane of all that on Earth I lovd
> My Brother starvd between two walls
> His Childrens Cries my Soul appalls
> I mockd at the wrack & grinding chain
> My bent Body mocks their torturing pain
> Thy Father drew his sword in the North
> With his thousands strong he marched forth
> Thy Brother has armd himself in Steel
> To avenge the wrongs thy Children feel

> But vain the Sword & vain the Bow
> They never can work Wars overthrow
> The Hermits Prayer & the Widows Tear
> Alone can free the World from fear
> For a Tear is an Intellectual Thing
> And a Sigh is the Sword of an Angel King
> And the bitter groan of the Martyrs woe
> Is an Arrow from the Almighties Bow
> The Hand of Vengeance found the Bed
> To which the Purple Tyrant fled
> The Iron hands crushd the Tyrants head
> And became a Tyrant in his stead [E 489–90)].

Most blatantly, the main Moravian symbol of "The Grey Monk" is the mysterious reference to the side-wound of Christ. In Moravian belief, the side-wound was strongly connected to the female genitals and occupied a prominent place in the sexually oriented rites and activities during the Moravians' liveliest, most radical and heavily contested period in the mid eighteenth century.[20] Although it is not specifically stated that the blood trickling down the side of the monk originates in a side-wound, the sheer combination of side and blood gives us a hint of Blake's knowledge of this Moravian feature and of its significance in their church tradition. With its emphasis on the Christ-like wide wounds on the hands and feet of the monk, the scene also anticipates similar illustrations in the designs of *Jerusalem*, which will be discussed below.

Overall "The Grey Monk" is quite a complex poem and is not easy to analyze.[21] There are several ambiguous components, perhaps most of all the various names and figures. What, for instance, is the relation of the mother in the first line to the rest of the persons of the poem? Is she the wife of the monk's brother who "starv'd between two Walls"? Is he the same man as the father in the following stanza? Logically he is not, since there is no indication of a change in speaker or addressee from the previous stanza. Rather, he seems to be the father of the mother of the first stanza and accordingly it is also her brother who appears two lines further on; both men being staunch warriors. In spite of the futility of war and the monk's idealistic stance of Christian forbearance, an act of vengeance is carried out in the final stanza, seemingly by "the iron hand" of the steel-armed brother. But then who is the merciless Purple Tyrant that has his head crashed? All in all, the poem circles around the mysterious grey monk and his Christ-like atonement. Then what is his relation to the other characters in the poem? Is he merely Blake's general representation and mouthpiece of Christian/Moravian forgiveness of sins?

It is probably of quite some significance too that Blake could not let go of "The Grey Monk" and in the introduction to the third book of *Jerusalem* we find a similar poem inserted. However, this version is shorter, only consisting of seven stanzas and a total of 28 lines, as opposed to the original's nine stanzas and 36 lines.[22] Upon closer scrutiny we notice that only two stanzas from the earlier version are fully retained here: importantly, the Moravian stanza with the "side-wounds" and the penultimate one including the well-known line "For a Tear is an Intellectual Thing." Otherwise, here Blake underscores the contrast between war and the pacifist monk martyr by invoking a few of his typically negative figures: Gibbon, Voltaire and Rousseau. Prophesying war they treat the pacifist with appropriate hostility:

> "Thou lazy Monk," they sound afar,
> "In vain condemning glorious War:
> And in your Cell you shall ever dwell:
> Rise, War, & bind him in his Cell!" [9–12, E 202].

This is well in context with this section of *Jerusalem*; in the prose passage preceding the Monk poem on plate 52 the unrighteous activities of these three negations are discussed. To these Blake posits an antidote, the forgiveness of sins in Jesus, another nod to the Moravians with their clear emphasis on Christ and his atonement on the Cross. Perhaps we also find some of the answers to the questions above: Gibbon and Voltaire call the monk lazy and lambast him for "in vain condemning glorious War," and it is those two who, figuratively, put him in a cell. Or, rather, Voltaire and Gibbon invoke war to do the trick: "Rise, War, & bind him in his Cell!" This is the point where the monk starts bleeding and the stanza from the earlier version is inserted next. Satan then becomes the great avenger and tyrant by rending the Moral Law from the Gospel and "He forg'd the Law into a Sword / And spill'd the blood of mercy's Lord" (52: 19–20, E 202).

Remarkably then, it seems that Moravian ideas remained with Blake all through his life. His grand epic *Jerusalem* appears increasingly influenced by major Moravian concepts the more we find out about the Moravian background and learn how to interpret along these lines with their unconventional codes and connotations. This became evident at the recent "Becoming Blake" conference at the University of Manchester's Whitworth Art Gallery. As the delegates had the good fortune to be able to see the two excellent coinciding exhibitions "Mind Forg'd Manacles: Blake and Slavery" and "Blake's Shadow: William Blake and his Artistic Legacy" I was quite unexpectedly taken aback by the extraordinarily Moravian look of the crucifixion scene of *Jerusalem* plate 76.[23] I suddenly saw the design purely with fresh and new eyes, something like Wallace Stevens's "first idea" as it were.[24] However, I was not immediately able to point to any specific features, it was simply a striking overall impression.[25] Here was the typically clear Moravian emphasis of the wounded and bleeding hands and feet of Christ. This is not the place for another laborious analysis of *Jerusalem* in its entirety, but the conclusion at this point must be that late in Blake's artistic career a number of key concepts from various esoteric sources had merged to make up an almost perfect and coherent unity, even though we must not disregard how difficult the poem certainly is. That it includes several Swedenborgian ideas has already been discovered and discussed by various scholars.[26] Importantly, also the great Moravian input to the poem now has to be fully recognized. Not only did Blake, significantly, insert "The Grey Monk" poem at a crucial spot of the epic, at the start of the third book which is entitled and addressed "To the Deists"—even more striking is the position of the crucifixion illustration on plate 76; it is notably the plate preceding "To the Christians," the prequel to the fourth and last chapter. Moreover, in *Jerusalem* for the first time Blake incorporates the notion of Universal Love in the Brotherhood of Jesus on a grander scale, where the forgiveness of sins is the guiding principle, a typically Moravian idea.

However, a bit surprisingly, perhaps the most obvious evidence of the Moravian influence to Blake's thinking is to be found in *The Marriage of Heaven and Hell*. In one of the Proverbs of Hell, which as it seems has been completely overlooked by scholars and commentators, Blake shows great awareness of the Moravian veneration of the genitals: "The head Sublime, the heart Pathos, the genitals Beauty, the hands and feet Proportion" (10: 1, E 37). To emphasise the genitals in what would have been at the time a highly unfashionable and inappropriate way surely can have no other reason than a profound Moravian influence. It is all the more remarkable as *The Marriage* was produced rather early in Blake's career, 1790, and we know that as a whole it was quite an important poem to him, containing several of his basic ideas.

Returning to *The Pickering Manuscript,* the poem "Mary" is intriguing for several reasons. On one level, it is a comment on Blake's own life and his marginal position as a misunderstood artist and outcast, with the famous lines "O, why was I born with a different Face? / Why was I not born like this Envious Race?" (21–2, E 487). On another level, these lines can of course be applied to the eponymous protagonist of the poem. As many commentators have pointed out, the hostile and negative treatment she is exposed to certainly fits the behavior that Blake's friend Mary Wollstonecraft had to endure in her much too short life.[27] Through her passionate and loving personality and her open and generous attitude to friends and compatriots Mary gains instant popularity: "An Angel is here from the heavenly Climes / Or again does return the Golden Times" (5–6, E 487). Somehow the cup has overflowed the measure and next morning she is derided and scorned by the ones she thought were her friends: "Some said she was proud, some call'd her a whore / And some, when she passed by, shut to the door" (17–18, E 487). This is a sudden and rather unexpected reaction not only to Mary but also to the reader of the poem, and one wonders what may have caused it. Whatever it might be, this is the passage that is most clearly related to the radical female emancipatory views of Wollstonecraft and then most notably her ideas of "free love." Or, taken a bit further, Mary is simply too generous out of Christian love and forbearance. So on this broader perspective Blake throws harsh criticism upon mankind in general and Mary becomes the only true representation of the benevolent God: "She remembers no Face like the Human Divine" (43, E 488). All in all, she is caught up in an impossible circular catch 22 situation: whatever she does to conform to the ignorant society, it turns out wrong and she always ends up in the original position of castigation. Thus, a conventional and bigoted society cannot stomach her good example of free and Christian love and it is to no avail that poor Mary assumes a humble attitude:

> She went out in Morning attir'd plain & neat
> "Proud Mary's gone Mad" said the Child in the Street
> She went out in Morning in plain neat attire
> And came home in Evening bespatter'd with mire [33–6, E 488].

Supposedly, the contempt of the mob is something that radicals of all time have had to put up with, and it is not far-fetched that it is his outspoken fellow author that Blake identifies with throughout the poem and takes sides with in the final stanza:

> And thine is a Face of sweet Love in despair
> And thine is a Face of mild sorrow & care
> And thine is a Face of wild terror & fear
> That shall never be quiet till laid on its bier [45–8, E 488].

Most likely, these lines are to a great extent also autobiographical. That this is the case can be substantiated by Blake's use of the main idea of "Mary" in similar lines in his letter to Thomas Butts from August 16, 1803:

> O why was I born with a different face
> Why was I not born like the rest of my race
> When I look each one starts! when I speak I offend
> Then I'm silent & passive & lose every Friend
> Then my verse I dishonour. My pictures despise
> My person degrade & my temper chastise
> And the pen is my terror. the pencil my shame
> All my Talents I bury, and Dead is my Fame
> I am either too low or too highly prizd
> When Elate I am Envy'd, When Meek I'm despisd [E 733].

The most persistent theme of "Mary" is "madness" and people's reaction to it, and it is obvious that Blake was aware of his closest social environment's perception of him and that this is something that at times he found troublesome and caused anxiety. And, as we know, it is one of the most persistent circulating anecdotes about Blake that he was mad. From Blake's own time we have for instance Robert Southey's familiar opinion of *Jerusalem*: when he saw Blake's epic poem in 1811, he condescendingly remarked to the diarist Crabb Robinson that it was "a perfectly mad poem" and that the author of the poem believed that "Oxford Street is in Jerusalem" (Bentley, *Blake Records*, 229).[28] But even with this frequently used anecdote we must be skeptical of its authenticity. The statement does not, as most people would believe, originate in Southey's own words but, rather, in a diary entry by Henry Crabb Robinson from July 24, 1811, where he writes that Blake "showed S. a perfectly mad poem called Jerusalem" (Bentley, *Blake Records*, 310). Furthermore, we cannot be sure exactly what Southey meant by "mad" here since he obviously had quite an ambiguous opinion of Blake as something of an insane genius, and some time after Blake's death he referred to him as "[t]hat painter of great but insane genius, William Blake" *(The Doctor,* 1847, VI, 116–17, in Bentley, *Blake Records*, 300). It is, however, clear that Southey linked

Blake's very special geniality with madness. In a letter to Caroline Bowles from May 8, 1830, he wrote: "Much as he is to be admired, he was at that time so evidently insane, that the predominant feeling in conversing with him, or even looking at him, could only be sorrow and compassion" (Bentley, *Blake Records*, 530). To take another example concerning Blake's "madness" involving a fellow author, there is Charles Lamb's written reply of May 15, 1824, to a friend enquiring about Blake, whose poem "The Chimney Sweeper" of *Innocence* he had been greatly intrigued by. Lamb informs him that he is not sure if Blake is still alive and continues, "for the man is flown, whither I know not, to Hades, or a Mad House — but I must look on him as one of the most extraordinary persons of the age" (Bentley, *Blake Records* 393–94). Although it is doubtful that any literary commentator or well-informed person today would seriously believe that Blake was truly insane, the early anecdotes have been perpetuated throughout the years, together with similar dubious anecdotes contributing to our uncertain and unstable picture of the great poet.

With "The Crystal Cabinet" we return to Blake's most sexualized symbolism. The speaker of the poem, in a cheerful mood and receptive state of mind, is enchanted by a newfound temptress:

> The Maiden caught me in the Wild
> Where I was dancing merrily;
> She put me into her Cabinet
> And Lock'd me up wit a golden Key [1–4, E 487].

The cabinet of course stands for the female genitals and in the following stanza we get a colorful description of this wondrous place:

> The Cabinet is form'd of Gold
> And Pearl & Crystal shining bright
> And within it opens into a World
> And a little Moony Night [5–8, E 487].

We hereby enter the world of Beulah, the third level of Blake's mythology, where sexual feelings find their natural expression:

> Another Maiden like herself
> Translucent, lovely, shining clear
> Threefold each in the other clos'd —
> O, what a pleasant trembling fear! [13–16, E 487].

Presumably, this sense of fear arises from the tension and excitement of illicit love. The feelings are reciprocated and, most interestingly, the male speaker attempts to reach an even higher level:

> I strove to sieze the inmost Form
> With ardor fierce & hands of flame
> But burst the Crystal Cabinet
> And like a Weeping Babe became — [21–4, E 487–88].

To me, there seem to be two interpretations of this sequence. First, on the sexual level, as intercourse continues the male endeavors for his penis to penetrate more intensely and deeper into the vagina but ultimately fails and ejaculates prematurely, bursting the cabinet. On the mythological level, it appears as if Blake somehow, through the intensity of sexual intercourse, envisions his fourth level of Eden. However, by the premature ejaculation the attempt fails. Most intriguingly, this would imply that Blake considered the mutually fulfilled sexual act as a means to, however briefly, reach his highest visionary level. This becomes even more plausible and logical in the last stanza as both man and woman are equally negatively affected by the unfulfilled sexual intercourse:

> A weeping Babe upon the wild
> And Weeping Woman pale reclin'd
> And in the outward air again
> I fill'd with woes the passing Wind [25–8, E 488].

There are a number of links between "Mary" and the final Pickering poem "William Bond." For one thing, they both deal with clandestine love-affairs, or at least intentions of ones. Moreover, we can find reverberations of Mary Wollstonecraft in the latter poem too. Just like Mary of the former poem, the main character William Bond finds himself in great distress because of his indulgence in excessive emotions of love:

> He went to Church in a May morning
> Attended by Fairies one, two & three;
> But the Angels of Providence drove them away
> And he return'd home in Misery [5–8, E 496–97].

A little further on Blake mixes components from his own sphere with that of Wollstonecraft's. The name William Bond naturally indicates a close relation to the writer with the same initials. Can we be sure, then, that Blake here refers to his own circumstances and his marriage to Catherine? There are a number of components that fit in well with his life: The obsession with love and marital relations during this period, the desperation and admonitions from Catherine, her extreme reaction by falling ill. We know that Catherine was in quite poor health for much of the time at Felpham, and this certainly fits with Mary Green of the poem. But William Bond's wife is not Catherine, but Mary Green. Not only does this make us think of Wollstonecraft but there are also resonances from her frank sexual and at the same time humble attitude, as for instance seen in "Mary," when she once suggested that she could take the place as servant in Henry Fuseli's household:

> O William, if thou dost another Love
> Dost another Love better than poor Mary
> Go & take that other to be thy Wife
> And Mary Green shall her Servant be [21–4, E 497].

There is a clear link between Wollstonecraft and Blake here in the form of the anecdote that he once proposed to Catherine that they take a handmaiden into their household. Less well-known is Blake's claim to Crabb Robinson, remarkably as late as 1826, that he "had learned from the Bible that wives should be in common" (Bentley, *Blake Records*, 704–05). This idea could of course also have been picked up from the Swedenborgians, and then particularly their intended expedition to Sierra Leone. And yet again it seems as if this was indeed a troublesome period in the married life of the Blakes, with William Bond confessing that there is another woman in his life:

> Yes, Mary, I do another Love
> Another I Love far better than thee
> And Another I will have for my Wife
> Then what have I to do with thee? [25–8, E 497].

This completely reverses the situation and instead of William it is now Mary who is taken ill. There are further common denominators with "Mary" in the poem — madness, angels, a difficult and ultimately hopeless situation — which aid to support my suggestion that the ingredients of "William Bond" are a mixture of different biographical circumstances.

The ultimate message of "William Bond" appears to be that, as always in Blake, love is a mutual responsibility and the poem, and the whole *Pickering Manuscript*, finishes with his view of the true core of Christianity:

> Seek Love in the Pity of others' Woe
> In the gentle relief of another's care
> In the darkness of night & the winter's snow
> In the naked & outcast, Seek Love there! [49–52, E 498].

So then, what made Blake leave these challenging poems aside instead of continuing to work on them by adding designs and completing them in his illuminated method? Perhaps we can derive some clues from Bentley's comments on them. For one thing, Bentley gave them another overall title: the *Ballads Manuscript,* due to the paper they were written on, the abandoned sheets of Blake's patron William Hayley's *Ballads* (Bentley, *Blake's Writings*, 1733). This verifies the date that Blake transcribed them into fair copies as 1805 or shortly after. Concomitantly, and in line with my discussion here, I believe there could be two plausible reasons for Blake's subsequent neglect of these poems. Firstly, as nearly every poem in *The Pickering Manuscript,* and in the 1800–1803 *Notebook,* confirm, there were more or less serious domestic problems in the Blake household around the time of composing and transcribing them. Could it be that because of these marital hardships Blake was in deep need of some relief and quite simply wrote these poems as a kind of therapy? In that case, they had fulfilled their purpose after completion, albeit in a refined stage, and Blake saw no reason to labor with them any further. Secondly, as has also been implied in my discussion, these were years that saw considerable creative changes in Blake's art and poetry. As so many commentators have pointed out, there occurred some drastic change already around 1795 as Blake began to develop his mythology in new directions at quite some length and density. *The Four Zoas* is of course the starting-point of this but, as we have every reason to assume, he was not entirely happy with the result and therefore abandoned that poem. It is only with *Milton,* and later *Jerusalem,* that he fully immerses himself in the creation of a grand epic. As we know, this came to be a most daunting task; intimations of this may for instance, be found in the extremely scarce biographical information about Blake during those years, from roughly 1808 to 1820 — that is the years he made the two epics. It was a most exacting task that took its psychological and emotional toll on both Blake and his faithful wife, so there is good cause to believe that he simply did not have enough creative power to deal with any other major projects, including the Pickering poems.

Blake's Utopian "Colony"

By scrutinizing the three great prophecies it is clear that Blake visualized a utopian existence of equality as the outcome of these poems, something that mankind must aim for in the mundane every-day existence. The three prophecies are of course "only" artistic creations, but we know that on at least one occasion Blake became to some degree practically involved with a factual project to establish a community largely based on many of the components of his epics, a utopian colony, as it were. And again, the unique Swedenborgian four-day conference in 1789 at East Cheap was the event where this took place.[1]

The East Cheap conference appears to have been a most productive gathering, with several prominent and remarkable people joined together for four days. "Many Lovers of the Truths contained in the said Writings, from different Parts of the Kingdom, and from abroad, attended accordingly," Robert Hindmarsh writes in the minutes of the meeting (3). In one of the chief documentations of the conference in the British Library (London: British Library 1578.4020) J. R. Boyle in "Historic Notice of the Early Conferences" explains:

> The first Conference met on Monday, the 13th April, 1789, and continued its sittings till Friday, the 17th April. The Conference was principally occupied in assenting to a series of 31 doctrinal resolutions. In the minutes of the Great East Cheap Society, however, an account of the proceedings of this Conference is entered, which gives considerable information, additional to that contained in the printed Minutes [xix].

Boyle then goes on to give an account of the proceedings at the conference by transcribing the record from the Great East Cheap minute book. Most importantly, we can immediately find out important facts of the admission and the participation:

> The Conditions of Admission, were to subscribe the following Paper, viz.:—[xx] "We whose Names are hereunto subscribed, do

each of us approve of the Theological Writings of Emanuel Swedenborg, believing that the Doctrines contained therein are genuine Truths, revealed from Heaven, and that the New Jerusalem Church ought to be established, distinct and separate from the Old Church. "Persons who subscribed, besides the 77 who signed the circular Letter*: —[xx].

Then follows a list of these intriguing names, eighteen in all: "Augustus Nordenskjold. Charles Harford. John Child. Frederick von Walden. Daniel Banham. Benj. Carpenter. C. Barrell. Josh. Richards. H. S. Barthelemon. Thos. Carter. Jno. Aspinshaw. R. Beatson. W. Blake. C. Blake. Dor. Gott. John Haywood. Thomas Scott.— Harman."[2] Accordingly, there could have been as many as 95 delegates at the conference. Unfortunately, we cannot be sure exactly who did eventually participate, but for the eighteen subscribers above.[3]

The difficulty to come to accurate terms with the specifics of the conference participation is obvious in David Worrall's treatment of the issue. In the account in his paper "Thel in Africa" of some of the most interesting delegates we can notice a mixture of names from the two lists. Most of them are to be found among the conference subscribers: Augustus Nordenskjöld, Francois Barthélemon, Colborn Barrrell and John Aspinshaw. Robert Jackson, on the other hand, is among the 77 signers on the other list, and so, quite remarkably, is the conference co-organizer himself, C. B. Wadström. And where on these lists can we find Barthélemon's wife Maria? Surely also Robert Rix is off the mark when claiming that 56 of these 77 were actual members, while the other 18 only signed as sympathizers. Importantly though, as Rix also states, the last-mentioned group, among whom were the two Blakes, did not commit themselves to become members of the Church (48).

Notwithstanding, several of the 95 potential delegates were people with intriguing backgrounds, well worth a closer look. Among the people that Blake and his wife met at the Swedenborg meeting were the president of the conference, Henry Peckitt, who is said to have had a large collection of rare mystical books; the violinist, freemason and conductor at the Royal Opera House, Manoah Sibley, an autodidact former Baptist, bookseller of Swedenborg's works and the occult sciences; Francois Barthélemon; his wife Maria[4]; the American merchant/agent Colborn Barrell; the Jamaican judge Robert Jackson, who was most likely involved in the control of the slave plantations in that country; the Holborn smith

John Aspinshaw, who was one of the subscribers to the first edition of the ex-slave Olauduh Equiano's *Interesting Narrative*[5]; and the two Swedes August Nordenskjöld and Carl Bernard Wadström.[6] These two had come to London in the years preceding the conference as part of a project to bring several of Swedenborg's manuscripts with them from Sweden, where they had just been banned in an upsurge against the Swedenborgians by the Swedish government. Wadström had been the president of the Swedish Swedenborg society, the Exegetical and Philanthropic Society *(Eksegetiska och Philantropiska Sällskapet),* founded in 1786 by August Nordenskjöld's brother Carl Frederick. With his radical and reformist political views, Wadström quickly became a leading member of the London Swedenborgians. August Nordenskjöld, on the other hand, in similarity to Swedenborg, had a background as a mineralogist but had soon turned his interest to alchemy, which he linked to Swedenborg's writings as a means to radically improve the world. The French pharmacist and surgeon, high-ranking Mason and Hugenot Benedict Chastanier is another person of interest. He was a major name in the London Swedenborgian milieu at this time and translated several of Swedenborg's works into French, including a plan for a Universal Swedenborgian Society. "Throughout the 1780s, Chastanier and his Universal Society had a profound influence on the reception of Swedenborg's teachings," Rix states (87). Rix further claims that the Universal Society with Chastanier made up the foundation of Swedenborianism at the time Blake attended their first conference at Great East Cheap (89). Chastanier also had a well-developed international network and together with French Swdenborgians he founded a quasi-masonic society of "Illuminés theosophes" (Hessayon, 31). More importantly, Chastanier had strong connections with the Berlin Masonic group the Illuminati. Intriguingly, these had a profound interest in alchemy, astrology and the Kabbalah, which were becoming fashionable topics in radical religious circles at the time (Hessayon, 33). But perhaps the most fascinating person of them all was Dorothy Gott. She was something of a prophetess and a striking example of women taking part in visionary experiences. Gott was part of "a distinct female tradition of British millenarianism whose roots lay in the radical sectarian challenges of the 1640s," according to Susan Juster in *Doomsayers* (216). For one thing, Gott is supposed to have been standing naked in her window to receive the true power of God in order to conjure up spirits. Of her spiritual awakening, Dorothy Gott herself writes: "These things strengthened me very much: I received great power to sing, and mighty things opened in that, as if a book was opened, and great light, which enlarged the meaning according to the promise" (Gott, 65–6). While discussing female visionaries in the vein of Joanna Southcott, Lynn Abrams in *The Making of Modern Woman* describes Gott as the British visionary "who renounced housework for the work of the soul" (38). Indeed, her prophecies have a remarkable down-to-earth quality overall.

Bearing in mind their many similar interests, we can be comfortably sure that Blake not only saw these persons but also took part in intriguing discussions with them, as David Worrall has convincingly claimed. It adds further to the likelihood of the argument that the utopian colonial venture was one of the plausible topics of the conference that an abridgement of Swedenborg's seminal work *Conjugial Love* entitled *A Sketch of the Chaste Delights of Conjugal Love, and the Impure Pleasures of Adulterous Love* is believed to have been printed only weeks before the publication of Wadström's *Plan for a Free Community* in late June 1789. It is Worrall's claim that both William and Catherine Blake eagerly partook in these discussions ("Thel," conference paper 8).[7]

One of the topics in common at the conference was slavery. Most likely this was the most pivotal matter for the aims of the Swedenborgians at this particular point in time. The focus on the African continent can be traced back to Swedenborg's belief that Africans had retained the clearest intuition of God. There was also the general notion that the lost books of the Bible were hidden somewhere in Africa. It was the urge to find these that led a number of Swedenborgian explorers to undertake some of the first expeditions to the west coast of Africa, with the intention of continuing to the heart of the continent where the books were presumably located. As David Worrall has suggested, it is most likely that Blake discussed these ideas with other delegates at the convention, most notably the two Swedes Nordenskjöld and Wadström.

Certainly, slavery was one of the most urgent issues for radicals in general during the 1790s. With the rise and steady growth of the British Empire, the slave-trade had become a natural ingredient to the establishment of the country, and it was only in 1807 that the slave-trade was finally abolished in Britain. Marcus Wood points to the social and cultural significance of slavery in his study *Slavery, Empathy and Pornography*:

> From the late 1780s until 1807, when the bill abolishing the British slave trade was finally passed, there was an explosion of material

on the subject. Race theory, the English conception of Africans and the English perception of Atlantic slavery, was suddenly transformed by propaganda in irreversible ways [141].

Interestingly, Wood goes on to tell us that at that time there also occurred an important shift in the concept of race-indication: "It was only during the last quarter of the eighteenth century that skin color emerged as the most significant indicator of race" (142). This fact is imperative for our understanding of Blake's treatment of slavery and the inclusion of black characters in his art and poetry, notably the little black boy and the illustrations to Stedman's *Narrative*. Naturally, it also has a bearing on the way we see Equiano and Peter Panah (dealt with below), as opposed to the way people perceived them at that time.

Blake, as we know, was much concerned with slavery at that time. For one thing, one of the major themes of *Visions of the Daughters of Albion* is slavery, and more commentators have probably read it in this way than with a gender focus.[8] As we shall soon see, it is also possible to read *The Book of Thel* with a slavery and colonial context. Remarkably, such a reading reveals that Blake showed an interest in slavery issues earlier than was previously believed as *Thel* was already printed in 1789. This is also the year of the Great East Cheap conference, which is the other substantial piece of evidence of this interest. According to Worrall, *Thel* is, for one thing, a critique of the predominant patriarchal components in the Swedenborgian colonial project as stated in Wadström's *Plan*. There is good reason to believe that the title of the poem is Blake's satiric allusion to Martin Madan's *Thelyphthora; Or, A Treatise on Female Ruin, in its Causes, Effects, Consequences, Prevention, and Remedy* from 1780. Here and elsewhere Madan enthusiastically propagated for polygamy. Most unfortunately, neither did he consult any women on the matter nor did he consider it possible for a woman to have several husbands. This was of course quite unacceptable to Blake with his innate ideas of human equality, and since the Swedenborgian project also had an obvious patriarchal slant with a tendency towards male polygamy, he shrewdly criticized the project through the satire in *The Book of Thel* (Worrall, "Thel" conference paper 14).

In Blake studies, slavery is traditionally considered to have come into Blake's philosophy and to have begun to form a major theme in his art and poetry in the early 1790s with the above-mentioned *Visions*. Further proofs of Blake's interest in slavery in the 1790s are his highly suggestive illustrations to his friend John Gabriel Stedman's *Narrative* from 1796.[9]

Most remarkably, these illustrations predominantly show the African inhabitants in a positive light, sort of having the upper edge of and being more lively and humane than the colonizers. As we have seen, in his recent article "Thel in Africa" David Worrall has managed to make even further connections in this issue. In an early draft of the essay, presented at the "Blake in the Orient" conference in Kyoto, Worrall suggests "that Blake knew of Peter Panah, [...] and that he incorporated an idea of the ex-slave in his *Song of Innocence*, 'The Little Black Boy'" (6). Panah was a black African slave released and taken care of by the Swedenborgian philanthropist C. B. Wadström.[10] Wadström brought Panah to London and set out to educate him, but unfortunately the wet and chilly English climate was more than he could bear and he died not even a year later. Wadström educating Panah is the motif of a painting by the portraitist Carl von Breda, well-known in both Britain and Sweden, who lived in London at that time.[11] The portrait was displayed at the Royal Academy in the momentous year 1789 in which Blake first printed *Songs of Innocence*, which makes it quite likely that Worrall is right that Blake saw it and that Peter Panah is indeed "The Little Black Boy." Black people were, after all, not an everyday phenomenon in the London of that time and it is not implausible that Blake took inspiration from the painting.

Worrall traces this back to the plans to set up a Swedenborgian utopian community in Sierra Leone on the west coast of Africa, on the initiative of Wadström and his Swedish compatriot August Nordenskjöld. "[T]he issue most engaging the church's activists was Wadström's Sierra Leone project," Worrall claims ("Thel in Africa," 41). The basic aim of the project as proposed in the *Plan* was the ensuing abolition of slavery and the intention was that the native Africans should live in equal harmony together with their "colonizers." That would also eventually bring about the abolition of "civil slavery" in Europe. This combined solution must certainly have been attractive to Blake, a view which Rix supports: "Blake sees slavery not only as an African problem, but as a general state of ignorance to the true ideal of Christian charity and brotherhood" (118). Remarkably, the civil life of the proposed colony was to use Swedenborg's idea of marriage as its governing maxim: "[T]he political economy of the colony was to be run entirely on the principles of conjugal love as outlined by Swedenborg" (Worrall, "Thel," 42). We can easily verify this by consulting Wadström's *Plan for a Free Community:* "This Government must exactly resemble a Marriage, which consists of two distinct Powers, the Active on the part of the Husband, and the Re-active on the part of the Wife" (*Plan*, 20). To begin with, we should note Wadström's interesting choice of words here: he does not follow the convention to call the female sex passive but re-active. This may have given Blake greater impetus to view woman as more active than contemporary tradition made out. Even more amazingly, and something that would have appealed to someone with a Moravian upbringing, was that sexual intercourse had to be performed on a regular basis in order to be a good citizen, as Worrall points out: "What was so uncompromising about the proposed 1789 Sierra Leone colony was that the sexual act was to be incorporated into its citizenship" ("Thel," 46). More specifically, this is what the *Plan* states: "The true exercise of civil duties is founded in an unboundedly active Industry, in what is useful; and true Religion, in an unlimited exercise of regular Conjugal Life" (*Plan*, xi). Further, even more clearly and crudely put, it was the husband's duty to "keep sacred Union with his Wife, by a diligent observance of the ultimate endearment" (*Plan*, 28). As Worrall so fittingly concludes: "The extent to which Blake's own beliefs intersect with Wadström's principles of citizenship founded upon the exercise of 'the ultimate endearment' within marriage is both striking and complex" ("Thel," 48). Most certainly, Blake must have been acquainted with the *Plan*, as it was well advertised in 1789 and 1790 in Swedenborgian publications, and he would presumably have taken interest in the project.[12]

Worrall takes it a step further and uses *The Book of Thel* as evidence for a connection between radical views of sexuality and utopian idealism among the Swedenborgians, and ultimately in Blake. "It is the sexual politics of this encounter with an uneasy combination of utopian idealism and Swedenborgian missionary zeal which is debated in *The Book of Thel*" ("Thel," 46). If we read *Thel* with these preconceptions in mind, radical sexuality and utopian idealism is quite a plausible combination. Some of the symbols lend themselves willingly to such an interpretation. In the previous chapter I have already discussed the ones with most obvious sexual connotations. The references to some titillating colonial adventure rather take the form of covert implications throughout the poem, and are not always easy to detect. It is only as we reach the final plate, part IV, that these aspirations become relatively outspoken: "The eternal gates' terrific porter lifted the northern bar: / Thel enter'd in and saw the secrets of the land unknown" (6: 1–2, E 6). As Thel now has entered into the new unknown territory "[s]he wander'd in the land of clouds thro' valleys dark, list'ning / Dolours & Lamentations" (6: 6–7, E 6). David Worrall conducts such a reading and comes to the intriguing conclusion that Thel's ultimate refusal to enter the experience of sexuality offered her throughout the poem is a symbolic renunciation of the Swedenborgian doctrine of conjugial love promoted by Wadström in his *Plan for a Free Community:*

> *The Book of Thel*'s structure, which is constructed around a narrative of her modes of refusal, can be contextualized with reference to Swedenborgian principles of conjugal [sic] love and their proposed west African colony. Thel's refusals are a rejection of her co-option into a community founded upon such principles ["Thel," 40].

If we subscribe to Worrrall's interpretation, then this would mean that, interestingly, we have some well hidden evidence of Blake's repudiation of Swedenborgianism's (in his view) too patriarchal and gender unequal principles, and his ensuing distancing from the New Jerusalem Church and Swedenborgian ideas for quite some time.

At the time of creating *Thel* in 1789 Blake seems to have been already aware of the negative ramifications of patriarchal social hierarchies, as Worrall makes clear: "Blake's own belief in the transcendent potential of 'sensual enjoyment' may sound like Swedenborgian 'Conjugal [sic] Love,' yet *The Book of Thel* makes it clear that Blake was aware of the patriarchal implications of such doctrines" ("Thel," 48). Therefore, read in this way *Thel* is a stinging satire of the proposed Sierra Leone colony and "[e]verything about Thel suggests that she is 'Anti-conjugal [sic]'" (Worrall, "Thel," 48). Finally, compared to other contemporary utopian colonial projects *Thel* presents a more sensible and down-to-earth impression. As David Worrall aptly sums up the discussion:

> [T]he whole point of *The Book of Thel* is that it does not posit a utopia but a practical "Vale of Har" which, as it proved, was rather more thoroughly elaborated and implemented than Coleridge and Southey's "Pantisocratic" community on the Susquehanna River, Pennsylvania, although, as one might expect, the moments of their political and ideological inceptions are broadly coincident ["Thel," 55].

Hence, the notion of slavery, or rather the abolitionist movement, was for the Swedenborgians and for some other distinguished radicals inevitably linked to the vision of a utopian existence in another continent.

As we notice above, a comparison with Coleridge and Southey's proposed Pantisocracy project is close at hand. This was an even more idealistic project instigated by the two poets at an early stage of their acquaintance in 1794. Just like the Swedenborgian project it never materialized and, again in similarity with the Swedenborgians, that was mainly due to irreconcilable differences in the view of sexual politics. And as much as this made Southey and Coleridge part company, it is most likely that Blake parted company with the Swedenborgians and their ideas for quite a while due to discrepancies in opinions of sexual and gender equality. The Swedenborgians around that time were simply too patriarchal, even chauvinist, for his taste. "[W]hile there is much to suggest that several aspects of Swedenborg's visualization of conjugal love were attractive to Blake, he immediately saw its basic flaw as being its lack of incorporation of women," as Worrall explains ("Thel," 52).[13]

Interestingly, further connections can be made with the Unitarians and their leading figure Joseph Priestley. He also aimed to set up a utopian community at the Susquehanna River after he had immigrated with his family to the New World. His pioneering attempts stood as an inspiration to Southey and Coleridge. This is how Ruth Watts describes Priestley's project:

> Of course, his emigration was in itself a political statement, as was the colony he hoped to establish in north-central Pennsylvania. [...] Soon there were to be settled in the area a community of like-minded Englishmen, politically and theologically liberal, escaping from persecution in England, for which Priestley was to be pastor and schoolmaster. This was the justification for the land-speculation venture of Thomas Cooper, Joseph Priestley Jr., William Russell, and others, optioning land between the west and northeast branches of the Susquehanna River ... [Watts, 329].

Priestley's colony was also never realized.

In many ways, perhaps, the most natural link in the colonial issue is to the Moravians. Of all the non-conformist congregations they showed the most missionary zeal, as I pointed out earlier on, and in due course they were to be established all around the world. Even today we find the Moravians generously represented world-wide in nearly every corner of the globe.

At the backbone of this analysis is the apocryphal Biblical Book of Enoch. Although the first modern translation of Enoch only appeared in 1821, a partial translation was published in 1715 and there was an increase of interest in this little-known text through James Bruce's rediscovery of it in 1773, narrated in his *Travels to Discover the Source of the Nile* from

1790. Since Enoch counts among the great apocalyptic literature, there is little doubt that Blake took great interest in the discovery. More importantly, it was this discovery that triggered some of the Swedenborgians to believe that there were still several undiscovered apocryphal books to be found somewhere in the heart of Africa. This was one of the main intentions of the colonial mission to Sierra Leone that Nordenskjöld and Wadström proposed in their *Plan for a Free Community*. "The theological foundation for such an expedition came from Swedenborg's frequent assertion that Africans have retained the clearest intuition from God," as Worrall affirms ("Thel," 40).[14]

Somewhat in contradiction to Worrall's view, I would argue that there are also components in Wadström's *Plan* that indicate a willingness to aim for improved gender equality. One such example is this key passage, which has already been quoted above:

> The Conjugal [sic] Alliance of the Community, which is between the Sexes, or between the Understanding in the Man and the Will in the Woman; or, Man's Wisdom and Woman's Love, because upon this depends intirely [sic] the improvement of the very elements in all Communities, which are Marriages, or the Conjugal Unions, and not, either Man or Woman separately considered [29–30].

We find further arguments for an early feminist inclination among the Swedenborgians in Alfred Acton's introductory comments to *Conjugial Love*: "Thus since a married couple in heaven embody good and truth, they must inevitably play an equal role in their marriage. The fundamental principle of equality was thus established by Swedenborg, long before it began to be asserted by the feminist movement" (X). This is both contradicted and supported in Henry Crabb Robinson's first-hand account of Blake. In these rather late opinions of and views by Blake from 1811, the poet first appears to distance himself from some of Swedenborg's ideas: "*Swedenborg*. Parts of his scheme are dangerous. His sexual religion is dangerous" (Robinson, *On Books and their Writers*, 328). But a little further on in the text Blake seems to contradict himself about the same issue in Swedenborg — sex, equality and early feminism: "He says that from the Bible he has learned that *Eine Gemeinschaft der Frauen Statt finden sollte*" (Robinson, *On Books*, 337).[15]

With so little context it is difficult for us to fully comprehend and interpret these two brief expostulations. It may become somewhat clearer as we know that "sexual religion" is a concept in Blake's later works with a strongly negative implication. However, we would ideally like to think that he derived and distilled the more positive and life-affirming Swedenborgian propositions about sexuality and an improved situation for women in general. It has been my task in this book to demonstrate that Blake in fact did so to a greater extent than previously believed. Disregarding to what degree I have succeeded in this, Blake's attitude to Swedenborg in many ways remains ambiguous. Robert Rix wholly agrees here: "Swedenborgianism made an impression on Blake's writing that is yet to be fully realized" (47). So whatever my conclusion may be, one thing is for certain: More scholarly investigation is called for regarding this issue.

Though utopian colonial projects of the Swedenborgians were never realized and fully accomplished, the discussions at East Cheap might, after all, have given Blake valuable inspiration for his own future attempts to create a utopian existence of another kind. One thing is for certain: he must clearly have understood the pitfalls and drawbacks demonstrated by the patriarchal inclinations of Wadström and company and been fully aware of them as he set out to make his own utopias in a written and illustrated form. He was now certain of what he must avoid. He expresses the matter in the famous preface to *Milton:*

> I will not cease from Mental Fight
> Nor shall my Sword sleep in my hand
> Till we have built Jerusalem
> In England's green & pleasant Land [1: 13–16, E 95–6].

It is my argument here, then, that the Swedenborgian conference in 1789 left an everlasting impression on Blake, for better and for worse. He used this formative experience to build on in the following twenty years till he had finally achieved his goal in his masterpiece *Jerusalem*. It is perhaps also significant that in *Milton* and other works he emphasizes that his form of utopia, Jerusalem, is to be built in his own homeland of England. It is as if in this way he condemned the Swedenborgian project: There is no need to look elsewhere to build a better society. It is clearly Blake's conviction that the construction of an improved society should start at our own native shores.

What Blake most forcefully denounced, though, was the patronizing and potentially insulting treatment of women in the proposed Swedenborgian project. As we have seen, in spite of some promising ambitions of gender equality, the society-to-be in Sierra Leone unfortunately was still very much a male adventure lending an uneasy prerogative to men in certain circumstances. For instance, while men were allowed to take a concubine to substitute for a disabled or unresponsive wife, no such opportunity existed for women. It is easy to understand what Blake with his Moravian background felt about such rules. The Moravians seem to have been more sensible and progressive about overall female emancipation and participation in everyday society. The notion that the soul is female, the image of a female mother Jesua and various leading offices appointed to women in the congregation all made the Moravians more advanced in gender equality than the Swedenborgians.

We can surmise too that the mistreatment of, or at least unfairness towards, women was one of the stepping-stones that finally made the Swedenborgian expedition crumble. Gender appears to be the most sensitive issue whenever the outlines of an improved utopian-like society are discussed. The failure of Coleridge and Southey's pantisocrasy project is only one example of many. As in the proposed society of the two poets it seems that it is always a male mistake, where men suggest that the women should be sexually shared or, as in the Swedenborgian case, where men should be allowed to take mistresses, with no intention that the same be true for women.

Another most intriguing query that will never be properly answered is whether Blake himself at any stage was prepared to practically commit himself to take part in a utopian colonial adventure of the Swedenborgian kind. Was he, for instance, prepared to set off to Sierra Leone? And was he prepared to bring Catherine with him? Perhaps it was Catherine who put an end to such lofty schemes? Were perhaps the negative ramifications so sincere that he gave up such ideas and instead went on to create their artistic and mental equivalent? As much as the Swedenborgians had eventually proved a disappointment, he nonetheless gained impetus from them and the insight that his utopian society must find other forms and foundations. So if he was ever prepared to take practical action, instead he now discarded practicality and matter-of-factness completely in favor of mental creations. Whatever positive inspiration Blake had previously had on the theoretical level by reading some of Swedenborg's theological works,[16] he was now put off by the practical utopian efforts of Wadström and his allies. Accordingly, it is very likely that it was this negative experience which made Blake distance himself from Swedenborg during a period of several years and even satirize him in his poetry. Significantly, the most biting satire of Swedenborg to be found in Blake's works appears shortly after the East Cheap conference in *The Marriage of Heaven and Hell*, most likely produced in 1790. It is here that Blake writes with such scorching irony: "As a new heaven is begun, and it is now thirty-three years since its advent, the Eternal Hell revives. And lo! Swedenborg is the Angel sitting at the tomb: his writings are the linen clothes folded up" (3, E 34). Therefore, while being an immediately bad experience at the occasion of the East Cheap meeting, Blake gained decisive insight which served him well in the long-term perspective when creating his major prophetic poems. It made him set off in new, hitherto unknown directions, in what was previously un-chartered territory in world art and literature.

Then, can we see any influence of the Swedenborgian kind of utopia on Blake's work after, say, *The Book of Thel*, which, if we are to follow Worrall's argument, represents his condemnation of the colonial project? Or, conversely, can we detect any reactions against the Swedenborgian ideas? Most definitely, *Visions of the Daughters of Albion* becomes an even more forceful indictment against the slave-like use of women if we take this background into account. Conducting such a double-focused reading of the poem will yield a powerful outcome.[17] The influence is noticeable already from the outset of the poem: "Enslav'd, the Daughters of Albion weep; a trembling lamentation / Upon their mountains, in their valleys, sighs towards America" (1: 1–2, E 45). The Daughters of Albion here presumably represent the Swedenborgian women who were to come along to Sierra Leone. They sigh for the freedom of America, but this is not going to be found in Africa. Instead the main protagonist Oothoon is raped by Bromion, who in this anti–Swedenborgian post-colonial reading might be a representative of the colonizers, that is Wadström et al. Bromion puts Oothoon in chains back to back to her pure and natural consort Theotormon. The two lovers are hereby prevented to take joy in each other by the patriarchal colonizer. In the much debated finale of the poem Oothoon exclaims that she cannot be forced to make love to a patronizing character like Bromion. Love must be voluntarily and freely enjoyed:

> But Oothoon is not so: a virgin fill'd with virgin fancies
> Open to joy and to delight where ever beauty appears
> If in the morning sun I find it, there my eyes are fix'd
> In happy copulation; if in evening mild wearied with work
> Sit on a bank and draw the pleasures of this free born joy
>   [6: 21–3 — 7: 1–2, E 50].

Thus, after a day's hard work in the colony Oothoon, or any of the other women, cannot be forced to make love with any patriarchs and figurative slave-owners, but will naturally seek out free spirits. Her fellow female colonizers join into her grief and laments: "The Daughters of Albion hear her woes & eccho back her sighs" (8: 13, E 51).

Significantly, the next poem in order in Blake's production is *America: A Prophecy*. Is this then a further development and comment on the Swedenborgian issue and colonization in general? As with *Visions* we are now a few years ahead in time, as both poems were created in 1793. By then Blake would naturally have digested the principles of Swedenborgian colonialism and moved on with his artwork, so that the immediate reactions had now found a more obscure and covert form in Blake's increasingly elaborate poetry. Still, I believe, *America* could well be concerned with these ideas to quite some extent. Instead of Sierra Leone we have America, Canada, Mexico and Peru.

One development in this poem is that for the first time we find Blake working with apocalyptical images: "The times are ended; shadows pass, the morning 'gins to break" (8: 2, E 54). This, as we know, was a concept that he was going to use in most of his subsequent poetry and refine into perfection in *Jerusalem*. However, here in *America* the use is very brief and sketchy, and Blake seems to not yet know how to naturally integrate his apocalyptic inclinations into the poem.

Even though *America* is a clear indictment of the negative effects of colonization, it is difficult to claim that it is a document promoting gender equality by defending the rights of female slaves in the more obvious way that *Visions* does. It is rather a general critique with Blake using the American battle for independence and its eventual positive outcome in the American Revolution as the backdrop and vehicle for his concern about the state of things in his native Albion's shore. However, some remnants of the other poem can be found as the permutations of the American warfare threaten to spread over the Atlantic:

> Then had America been lost, o'erwhelmed by the Atlantic
> And Earth had lost another portion of the infinite
> But all rush together in the night in wrath and raging fire
> The red fires rag'd! the plagues recoil'd! then roll'd they back with fury
> On Albion's Angels: then the Pestilence began in streaks of red
> Across the limbs of Albion's Guardian [14: 17–20 —15: 1–2, E 56].

The negative repercussions from America finally affect the institution of marriage, where the women are fettered "in bonds of religion," possibly referring to Swedenborgianism:

> The doors of marriage are open, and the Priests in rustling scales
> Rush into reptile coverts, hiding from the fires of Orc
> That play around the golden roofs in wreaths of fierce desire
> Leaving the females naked and glowing with the lusts of youth
> For the female spirits of the dead, pining in bonds of religion
> Run from their fetters reddening & in long drawn arches sitting
> They feel the nerves of youth renew, and desires of ancient times
> Over their pale limbs as a vine when the tender grapes appears
>   [15: 19–26, E 57].

Though the fetters here hark back to *Visions,* this passage also points forward in Blake's poetic production through its use of apocalyptic images like "tender grapes." Hence, *America* clearly is a transitional poem in Blake's oeuvre. Nonetheless, the poem is significant in that it is the first place where Blake makes material use of what was to be something of his stock, albeit supernatural, characters in the major prophecies. So, in *America* Urthona, Orc and Urizen are all introduced. Two of them are thrown in at the very beginning in the first line of the "Preludium": "The shadowy Daughter of Urthona stood before red Orc / When fourteen suns had faintly journey'd o'er his dark abode" (1: 1–2, E 51). Or, to be more precise, it is of course Urthona's daughter who is launched here. That this is a preliminary introduction is obvious since this character is what is later to become the Shadowy Female in *The Four Zoas* and *Jerusalem*. The first outright mention of Urthona occurs a little later: "anon a serpent folding / Around the pillars of Urthona" (1: 15–16, E 51). Urizen, significantly, is first mentioned at the earliest clear apocalyptic announcement in Blake's poetry, already indicated above: "The times are ended; shadows pass, the morning 'gins to break / The fiery joy, that Urizen perverted to ten commandments" (8: 2–3, E 54). Even at this early instance it is evident that Urizen is Blake's negative deity with the reference to the law-proclaiming God of the time of Moses.

    Blake's development of his illuminated method of writing and printing in *Visions* and *America* pushes another important aspect to the fore: The commercial potential of Blake's work at this time, and why it was never fully realized. As Robert Rix points out in his discussion of Blake's somewhat earlier abortive poem *The French Revolution* from 1791, there was great interest in and a reasonably big market for radical postmillennial works that envisioned an improved society at the outset of the revolution in France until 1792, when the great terror set in. We know that

Joseph Johnson agreed to publish Blake's proposed epic in seven books and that the first was printed but never put on the market. The reason for this has never been fully clarified but it is safe to believe that the political context was somehow too intimidating to risk the publication, whether it was down to Johnson, Blake or both. The title is after all *The French Revolution*, there is no beating around the bush or hiding from this fact. It is definitely a title that would not go down well with the British authorities from 1792 onwards. Rix's belief that Blake's poem suffered for the turbulence and repercussions after the publication of Burke's *Reflections on the Revolution in France* seems plausible. As he concludes: "It is possible that Blake's *The French Revolution* became a casualty in the campaign for respectability of Johnson and his associates" (151). Even more intriguing is the idea that it was Johnson's cancellation of this poem that made Blake realize that his poetry and art was so special and charged with poignant meaning that he had to do it all by himself through his illuminated printing. He had to do everything to conceal his many radical ideas through the sophisticated symbolism of his self-invented mythology. It is an exciting thought that works such as *America* and *Europe* may have found a bigger commercial market had Johnson only dared to print *The French Revolution*. These two poems were after all both subtitled *A Prophecy*, something which should have enabled them to have found a much wider audience considering the general demand in the times they were self-produced by Blake.[18]

By the time Blake gets to *The First Book of Urizen* he becomes preoccupied with other things and his unique mythological system begins to find its final shape. Enter here also Blake's alter ego Los, the poetic inspiration who is the closest we get to a hero in his poetry:

> And Los, round the dark globe of Urizen
> Kept watch for Eternals to confine
> The obscure separation alone
> For Eternity stood wide apart [5: 38–41, E 73].

We are now getting towards the end of Blake's transitional period but before he begins creating his three great epics there are a few more poems to come. *The Song of Los* appears to be another intermediary poem, in which Blake attempts a new two-part structure. Since he subtitles the two sections "Africa" and "Asia" we may assume that the colonial perspective is somehow continued in this poem, even if it is difficult to read anything substantial into it that points to the Swedenborgian project. That Blake has not quite settled his mythological scenery is indicated through his repetitive use of characters from previous poems such as Oothoon and Theotormon in *The Song of Los*. It seems that Blake was not confident enough to create new and more befitting characters. Next follow *The Book of Ahania* and *The Book of Los*. Neither of these two poems seems to be concerned with the issues dealt with at the East Cheap conference. Instead, sometime around 1795 the poems become more introverted and abstract and, as we know, their degree of complexity increased considerably. It is at this point that many commentators have stated that there is a more or less dramatic change in Blake's art and poetry. Blake is now ready to enter his magnificent mythological landscape.

So what does this widening scope of mythology imply for Blake's treatment of slavery issues? Can we discern any residual effects from the conference at East Cheap in *The Four Zoas, Milton* and *Jerusalem*? In a general sense there is an implicit critique towards all forms of repression in these poems. So though this critique is directed foremost towards the negative gender politics that allow one sex to repress the other, the mechanisms of gender repression are the same that allow master to repress slave, as Wollstonecraft had already pointed out by then.[19] Hence, as we know that there are many levels in Blake's major epics, the mistreatment of women as slaves is certainly there too with the crucial experience at the Swedenborgian meeting still lingering in the back of his mind. But the three great prophecies are so all-encompassing, sophisticated and refined that it has now become next to impossible to tell what is what and to point to specific examples of any one issue. However, considering its time of creation, it might be possible to argue that *The Four Zoas* could still have been more overtly concerned with slavery as a major issue since the slave-trade was not abolished until the Act of Parliament in 1807. By that time Blake had moved on artistically and was well into work on either *Milton* or *Jerusalem*, or both. In those two more stately poems it is difficult to pin down any certain references to slavery.

So, if we tackle the matter conversely, what inspiration did Blake draw from the East Cheap meeting for the depiction of a utopian existence in his three epics? What were the good bits that he could build on and develop? The foundation of the ideal Swedenborg society was, as we know, to be built on conjugal love in the form of marriage between equal man and woman. In Blake's three epics this is also emphasized symbolically through the ultimate goal of the reunion of male and female, which in different ways is the outcome of these poems.

Some of the names and symbols from Blake's most urgent treatment of the matter in *Visions of the Daughters of Albion* seem to be retained in the longer poems. The Daughters of Albion become the Daughters of Beulah as Blake attempts to emphasize sexuality in his third level of existence, Beulah. "The Daughters of Beulah, terrified, have clos'd the gate of the Tongue / Luvah & Urizen contend in war around the holy tent" (1: 479–80, E 311), Blake writes in *The Four Zoas*. Could the Daughters of Beulah refer back to the potentially repressed women who were to take part of the expedition to Sierra Leone? That may seem a long-shot but it cannot be completely ruled out that the negative implications of the colonial adventure still lingered in Blake's mind and resurfaced in the composition of the *Zoas*, though consciously or subconsciously is, of course, difficult to know. It would be next to impossible to unearth substantial evidence in this issue, so any such claim would inevitably only consist of conjectures.

Milton is in several aspects a different kind of poem. It is, as we know, the most personal of the three epics with Blake making comments on his own domestic situation through the vehicles of John Milton and his wives and daughters in the shape of the six-part character Ololon. This is indeed a very clever arrangement, but has the poem anything to tell us on a more universal level? Is the Swedenborgian conference hovering there somewhere, lurking at the back of things? The poem most definitely makes a strong comment on sexual politics, as we have already seen. Can the implied repression by John Milton of the women close to him be transferred to the universal level? The answer must surely be an emphatic yes, and it is not difficult to see Milton's women fettered as slaves. This is fine with the John Milton–implied level of symbolism, but where does this leave the domestic level with William and Catherine Blake? Can we read their situation as analogous to Milton's domestic problems? I believe this is more difficult to answer but as Blake is a truly omniscient and omnipotent author it should certainly be put into the equation — the one does not exclude the other. It would certainly add one more fascinating level to an already intricate and tantalizing poem.

As we come to *Jerusalem* we are elevated to a higher level, a level of greater universality and commonality, as it were. The degree of abstraction is also much more elevated than in *Milton* and *The Four Zoas*. Hence, *Jerusalem* is such a complex and elusive poem that it does not lend itself to such an explicit and precise interpretation.

Conclusion: "Moravian" Blake

This book has attempted, firstly, to enlighten the many important discoveries in Blake studies in recent years and, secondly, to use these new findings in the investigation of some appropriate poems in Blake's oeuvre. Aided by Keri Davies's and Marsha Keith Schuchard's crucial discoveries of the Moravian background of Blake's mother, I hope to have demonstrated a more profound Moravian influence on Blake's art and poetry than formerly recognized by scholars. I also hope to have shown a greater overall dependence on Swedenborgian features throughout Blake's complete work.

So, it is now established that Blake's family background was, at least on his mother's side, Moravian and that at some point there was a large input of Swedenborgian ideas in his immediate environment that came to deeply and continuously influence him. How, then, will these fundamental and compelling facts in turn influence us as Blake scholars, students, readers and enthusiasts?

To begin with, a great number of Blakean commonplaces, anecdotes and critical fallacies can now either be definitely dismissed or revaluated. The most important naturally concerns Blake's religious orientation. As I have demonstrated, he neither was of a very radical belief, nor was he a genuine dissenter. That his orientation indeed was of a particular mixture is another matter. Furthermore, and perhaps as importantly, we can now say that Blake was not a sexist. Rather, the central tenets of his religious mixture influenced him to strive for greater equality and an overall improved appreciation in society for women.

Secondly, a few other premises can now be corroborated, at best supported by new pioneering documentation. Linked to the above, Blake's sexual politics were in fact even more radical than previously believed, and definitely constituted the most radical component in his work and everyday life. Through many of his illustrations and several of his poems we have assumed that he extolled nudity, the male and female genitals and

Conclusion

the sexual act itself. In the unique basic notions of the Moravians and the Swedenborgians about these issues we now have very good support that this was indeed the case.

Thirdly, Blake studies can now be focused on fully worthwhile and productive issues. Even though the Moravian background of Blake's mother is now established, there are a lot of blind spots still to explore. While the fact about Blake's mother is an invaluable piece of information, it also raises new questions: what was the religious orientation of Blake's father? Was he also from a Moravian family? Is it correct to presume, analogously, that like Catherine's first husband Tomas Armitage he was of Moravian descent? What other connections to a Moravian surrounding were there in Blake's family? When, how and from where did Swedenborgianism enter his family? Was Blake's father James perhaps a Swedenborgian? Did Blake then naturally mix the Moravianism of his mother with the Swedenborgianism of his father?

What will the future of Blake studies look like then? Naturally, the focus should be linked to these questions and the number one priority must be to further verify and substantiate Blake's Moravian background, building on the breakthrough with the archival evidence of his mother's birthplace. This does not seem a too intimidating and wholly impossible task, given the vital lead we now have. It certainly should be possible to find out more about Blake's father, and Keri Davies, for one, is already searching various archives to make a similar breakthrough.

The Swedenborgian influence also needs further and more thorough investigation. There are many intriguing connections to various fascinating persons, particularly the ones taking part in the 1789 meeting at East Cheap. Danish Blake scholar Robert Rix has just published a full-length study focused mainly on Blake and Swedenborg, *William Blake and the Culture of Radical Christianity,* and I will myself pursue this line of investigation by searching archives and collections in Sweden, among other places. Presumably, due to language difficulties, these have not been properly analyzed before.

But the Moravian and the Swedenborgian influences are not the only tracks worth following in the next few years. Several other findings have been made in recent years which will alter our premises to various degrees and will provide great impetus and important starting-points for further research that could prove to be crucial for the elucidation of Blake as a person and artist.

For one thing, Keri Davies has managed to establish that the late eighteenth- and early nineteenth-century audience reading Blake was larger than previously believed. "Taken together, these new pieces of evidence should compel a revision of the established assumption that Blake lacked any significant contemporary audience," he claims in his article on the first female Blake collector Rebekah Bliss ("Mrs Bliss," 226). By scrutinizing letters between Richard Twiss and Francis Douce, Davies has also found evidence of a more numerous contemporary female readership of Blake, pointing to the collector Bliss. Also, David Worrall has suggested that Blake, at an early stage of the production of his prophetic works, intended these to reach a wider audience than they in fact did. Worrall sees such a potential in the monochrome printings made before Blake started producing the more expensive and elaborate color-printed works in 1794 and 1795. *Songs of Innocence and of Experience* is another work that, probably more naturally, had this commercial potential in the prevailing political climate.[1]

As mentioned earlier, David Worrall furthermore suggests a closer bond between Blake and certain Swedenborgian believers, whom Blake is supposed to have encountered at the East Cheap conference. Although he has already started to investigate a few of these relations, notably in the early draft of his essay "Thel in Africa," there is much exciting work to be done here. The prophetess Dorothy Gott is only one of several intriguing personalities to investigate.

Angus Whitehead has in his thorough research of Blake's different addresses managed to unearth many details of our poet's daily life that have never been thought of before. For instance, he has established that Catherine Blake's sister Sarah lived at their last residence at 3 Fountain Court, and was probably a major reason for them moving there. He also suggests that Sarah had a child, Louisa, by her husband, the landlord Henry Banes. This would mean that the Blakes were survived by a niece.[2]

We must also add to this of course the numerous new facts about Blake's printing, drawing and painting techniques put forth by scholars like Robert Essick, Joseph Viscomi, Michael Phillips and Mei-Ying Sung. Essick and Viscomi have both made invaluable contributions to our understanding of Blake's printing methods and artistic techniques: Essick in *William Blake, Printmaker* and Viscomi in *Blake and the Idea of the Book,* to mention a few of their works. Most recently, Viscomi has managed to establish the order of the illuminated books Blake produced in 1795: *The Book of Los, The Book of Ahania, The Song of Los* ("Blake's 'Annus Mirabilis'"). For highlighting and physically reconstructing the printing presses used by Blake in his time, Michael Phillips must naturally also be mentioned.[3] And lately Mei-Ying Sung has made important discoveries on the rectos of Blake's Job engravings, suggesting that Blake revised and corrected his work to a greater extent than what has been previously believed.[4] All this clearly points forward to the work that needs to be done relating to the designs of Blake; also, the work in this field is facilitated by and must take in the new findings of Blake's family background.

The overarching conclusion of this book is that we can now speak of Blake as a Moravian. His Moravianism is, as we have seen, to an undeterminable extent mixed up with some Swedenborgian and other ideas, but we can safely call him a Moravian.

All the same, my study also points to the need of intense further investigation in this issue. We need to establish to what degree we can say that Blake's religion was radical. What was his attitude and relation to the Church of England? More specifically, we must ask ourselves: How devoted a religious man was Blake? Most factors indicate that Blake was never actively, or in private, a committed adherent to any religious denomination, be it the Church of England or a faith of an antinomian kind. As we know so far, his only alleged immersion was to Swedenborgianism at the East Cheap convention. But since he never again, to our knowledge, participated in any organized Swedenborgian worship or other activity, I would not label him a Swedenborgian. In Blake's case I believe we should rather speak of him as a follower, or more correctly a user and modifier, of some Swedenborgian ideas. Hence, the evidence tells us that Blake's use of and attitude to Swedenborgian ideas is still undecided, but that there is substance enough to call him a Moravian.

The other conclusion of my book is that, with his unusual religious mixture as background and input, the foundation of Blake's thinking is sexuality. We have seen it in his appreciation of the most extreme expressions of a liberal and open-minded attitude towards love and sex. This has been shown in all three chapters on religion, sex and utopian colonies.

But perhaps the most important outcome of this book is that, whatever his religious orientation and view of sex and women, Blake's deeply humanist message is all about love. Love of man and of the divine in man, love of life and the earth that we live upon, of its plants and animals: "Everything that lives is holy." Everything that does not live is holy too. Inevitably then, all is of equal value in God's creation. And of course Blake is an advocate of complete equality of all kinds.

Chapter Notes

Introduction

1. See my previous study *William Blake and Gender* for a thorough discussion of these articles and other similar critical comments.

2. Tristanne Connolly, for instance, writes that "Bruder's book is a masterwork of new historicist criticism" (*William Blake and the Body,* xii). In the December 1997 *TLS* review Steve Clark fully recognizes Blake scholars' urgent need for Bruder's book, which he sees as "'a partisan exercise' by an 'active and resisting reader.'" As he claims, "Bruder ... makes an impressive contribution to a long-overdue revaluation of this tradition by demonstrating that Blake's indebtedness to popular culture, far from sustaining a revolutionary heritage, is at best mixed and problematic" (*TLS* 5 Dec. 1997). Nelson Hilton, in spite of being more sceptical overall, in his *Blake Illustrated Quarterly* review, calls it "[a]n at times interesting and provocative study" (*Blake/An Illustrated Quarterly* 32:1 [Summer 1998], 20).

3. Indeed, Hobson himself identifies three different critical diversions in the Blake and gender issue, and positions his own work between the first and the second but closer to the second, which he defines as a mixture of the two categories I have outlined above (*Blake and Homosexuality*, xiii).

4. The evidence has been put forth in various publications. See for instance Davies and Schuchard, "Recovering the Lost Moravian History of William Blake's Family," *Blake/An Illustrated Quarterly* 38 (2004), 36–43, Schuchard's *Why Mrs Blake Cried*, 13–14 and Davies's unpublished thesis, *William Blake in Contexts: Family, Friendships, and Some Intellectual Microcultures of Eighteenth- and Nineteenth-Century England,* 46.

5. Schuchard's source here is Nancy Bogen, "The Problem of William Blake's Early Religion," *The Personalist* 49 (1968), 509.

6. See Schuchard, *Why Mrs Blake Cried: William Blake and the Sexual Basis of Spiritual Vision*, 8–9 and 13.

7. However, for want of a more appropriate word I will use the term "radical" in my discussions of Blake and his context throughout the book.

Unitarians, Swedenborgians, Moravians

1. For this background information see Podmore, *The Moravian Church in England, 1728–1760,* 168.

2. Another critic who approves of the term "enthusiasm" in connection to Blake is Nicholas Williams. In the "Introduction: Understanding Blake" to his edition of the *Palgrave Advances in William Blake Studies* he discusses the eighteenth century use of the term and provides us with a definition:

The usual way of describing the generally working-class religious atmosphere from which Blake emerged is to label it "enthusiastic," by which is meant a dissenting Protestant, spiritualist, irrational (even if the members of the movement would not have used this word) and, from the point of view of the respectable middle-class, somewhat suspect religious excitability [2].

While I readily accept Williams's definition, I find it doubtful as to whether Blake's family were genuinely working-class, his father being a shop owner, and whether "enthusiasm" is a proper label for Blake's form of religion. In fact, it is linked to the main purposes of this book to demonstrate that this is probably not a suitable term.

3. See Davies, *William Blake in Contexts*, 46.

4. See my *William Blake and Gender*, 42–6, for a more extensive discussion of Thompson's Muggletonian argument.

5. According to K. D. Brown, *A Social History of the Nonconformist Ministry in England and Wales 1800–1930*, the five denominational groupings: Baptist, Congregational, Wesleyan, Primitive and United Methodist, had by 1900 claimed the allegiance of about 95 percent of all nonconformists. From his study he excludes denominations such as Presbyterianism (whose main geographical strength lay outside England and Wales), Welsh Calvinistic Methodists (whose membership was exclusive to small, limited areas) and Unitarians (as they were outside the prevailing evangelical orthodoxy and had fewer than 400 ministers in the nineteenth century). Brown makes no reference at all to Moravian ministers, as the largest listing of Moravian ministers serving in the British Province at any one time was 53 in the year 1870. I am grateful to Keri Davies for alerting me about this source.

6. Even though Wollstonecraft was to some degree inspired by Rousseau's views on education, it should be made clear that she strongly refuted his emphasis on a single-handed male education. This is particularly evident in her tract *A Vindication of the Rights of Woman*.

7. All references to the works of Blake in the text are from Erdman, ed., *The Complete Poetry and Prose of William Blake*, and are indicated by E.

8. Priestley's most foundational works on this are *The History of the Corruptions of Christianity* from 1782 and *History of Early Opinions Concerning Jesus Christ* from 1786.

9. In the chapter "International Swedenborgians in London" Robert Rix gives a valid survey of the radical context of 1780s and 90s London where the Swedenborgians became one of the most feared and shunned groups for some time. Rix puts this down to their close association with international lodges of Masons, who were feared as being part of the conspiracy theories that flourished after the French Revolution. "Up through the 1790s," Rix writes, "guardians of social order feared that so-called 'irregular' lodges of Freemasons would seduce English dissenters to take part in revolutionary plots." Due to this dubious connection the Swedenborgians were feared for all the wrong reasons and were believed to be more radical than they actually were, which is quite paradoxical bearing in mind the conservative turnaround of Hindmarsh and the Swedenborgians as a whole in the 1790s. They were even thought to be part of a pan-European revolutionary conspiracy, similar to the French one (Rix, 85). On the other hand, this picture conforms smoothly

with the overall social regress into blatant conservatism at the time, with an anxious and suspicious government taking all sorts of measures to hunt down radical and even liberal elements in society. See Rix, 85–105, for a survey of the radical international context of the London Swedenborgians. See also *William Blake and Gender*, 40–59, by the present author for a survey of the overall political and social context of England in the 1780s and 90s.

10. The expelled members were Hindmarsh, C. B. Wadström, August Nordenskjöld, Alexander Wilderspin, George Robinson and Henry Servanté.

11. See also Marsha Keith Schuchard, *Why Mrs Blake Cried*, 205–17.

12. See Rix, 123–28, for a similar discussion. Rix also deals with Blake's obvious parody and satire of Swedenborg in *The Marriage*, 128–34. Among other items, his examination contains an analysis of the crucial *Notebook* poem "I Saw a Chapel All of Gold", which is quite different from the one offered in this study. However intriguing Rix's point that the poem is a downright critique of the New Jerusalem Church may be, I find it somewhat odd that Blake would write such a poem in (presumably) 1793, several years after the break with the Church. Moreover, this interpretation of the poem does not go well with the sequence of the first six or seven *Notebook* poems. See 51–2 and 74-6 of this book. In line with this, Rix somewhat anticlimactically seems to refute his own point: "However, it would be misguided to conclude that Blake was writing pointed anti-New Church criticism in 1793. A more likely explanation for the allusions is that Blake had adopted Swedenborg's terminology, something he would continue to do in the following years" (134).

13. Rix has another idea: that it was Nordenskjöld's intention to find gold in order to undermine the economies of the European countries (97).

14. The Swedenborgian Library is located in the city of Linköping, some 50 kilometers west of Norrköping.

15. For an exhaustive survey of the life of Emanuel Swedenborg and his theosophy and sexual politics, see Schuchard, *Mrs Blake*, 59–121.

16. For an account of the life and work of Zinzendorf see Weinlick, *Count Zinzendorf*. See also Schuchard, *Why Mrs Blake Cried*, 15–22, for a brief survey of the life and theosophical ideas of Zinzendorf.

17. See for instance Colin Podmore, *The Moravian Church in England, 1728–1760*, 5 and E. R. Hasse, *The Moravians*, 9–12.

18. See Moravian Brethren, *History of the Unitas Fratrum*, 8–24, for an account of the origin and first period of the Moravian Church.

19. See Colin Podmore, *The Fetter Lane Moravian Congregation, London 1742–1992*, 5.

20. See Wienlick, 180.

21. See Geoffrey Stead, *The Moravian Settlement at Fulneck, 1742–1790*, 4.

22. See Podmore, *The Fetter Lane Moravian Congregation, London 1742–1992*, 12.

23. See Weinlick, 197.

24. "MORAVIANS NOT DISSENTERS." Letter to the editor of the Manchester Courier, *Manchester Courier* (May 29, 1872).

25. For this passage I am indebted to Podmore, *The Moravian Church in England*, 132–36; Atwood, "Sleeping in the Arms of Christ," 25–51; Schuchard, *Mrs Blake*, 32–3; and Davies, *William Blake in Contexts*, 297–307. For the sexual rites see also Schuchard, *Mrs Blake*, 48–54.

26. See Craig Atwood, "Sleeping in the Arms of Christ," *Journal of the History of Sexuality*, 35–36.

27. Blake and Zinzendorf are responding to the verses: Genesis 1:27: "So God created man in his own image, in the image of God created he him; male and female created he them" and Genesis 5:2: "Male and female created he them; and blessed them, and called their name Adam, in the day when they were created."

28. See Linda Colley, *Britons: Forging the Nation, 1707–1837*.

Blake's Religion

1. See Hindmarsh, *Minutes* and J. R. Boyle, "Historic Notice of the Early Conferences," ix-xl.

2. According to Rix, it is likely that Blake had already been introduced to London Swedenborgians by friends, of which John Flaxman is the most prominent and familiar suggestion. See Rix, 52-7.

3. Davies offers two English translations: "A literal English version would be:

> Nevertheless Blake belongs not to the Episcopal Church but from birth to a dissenting community; although we do not believe that he himself regularly attends at a Christian church.

Blake scholars tend to use Bentley's translation — apparently idiomatic, and it reads fluently enough:

> Nevertheless Blake does not belong by birth to the established church, but to a dissenting community; although we do not believe he goes regularly to any Christian church ["The Winepress of Love", 2].

4. See also Atwood, *Community of the Cross*, 178–83.

5. From *A Collection of Hymns, with Several Translations from the Hymn Book of the Moravian Brethren*, 49–50.

6. From *A Collection of Hymns Several by Several Authors. With Several Translation from the German Hymnbook of Ancient Morvian Brethren. For the use of several Religious Societies*. Hymn xxiii, final stanza, 35.

7. This passage reminds us of the apocalypse in Isaiah: "For the stars of heaven and the constellations thereof shall not give their light: the sun shall be darkened in his going forth, and the moon shall not cause her light to shine.... Therefore I will shake the heavens, and the earth shall remove out of her place" (13:10, 13:13). The version in Revelation is also close to Blake: "And I beheld when he had opened the sixth seal, and, lo, there was a great earthquake; and the sun became black as sackcloth of hair, and the moon became as blood; And the stars of heaven fell unto the earth, even as a fig tree casteth her untimely figs, when she is shaken of a mighty wind. And the heaven departed as a scroll when it is rolled together; and every mountain and island were moved out of their places" (6: 12–14).

Blake's Sexuality

1. The quote within the quote is from Rimius, *Candid Narrative*, 63. Moreover, we have visual evidence in Blake's sketch in *The Four Zoas* manuscript of a naked woman with genitalia transformed into a chapel. An erect penis forms a holy statue at the centre.

2. For some reason this exact variation of the poem is not found in Erdman, who instead includes a brief piece called "To my Mirtle" (E 469).

3. This phenomenon is what Jason Whittaker and Shirley Dent have labelled "appropriating Blake," something that they discuss at length in their book *Radical Blake*. In the last few decades it has become a common phenomenon in

Chapter Notes

popular culture to use Blake for various "kitschy" purposes in art and music. Whittaker and Dent point to the massive Blake exhibition at Tate Britain in 2000–1 as one recent relevant example of appropriation of the great artist. See Whittaker and Dent, 1–3. Whittaker discusses musical adaptations of Blake in "Mental fight, Corporeal War, and Righteous Dub: The Struggle for Jerusalem in Popular Music," an unpublished paper presented at the "Blake and Conflict" conference at Oxford University in September 2006.

4. See Mellor, "Blake's Portrayal of Women"; Ostriker, "Desire Gratified and Ungratified: William Blake and Sexuality"; and Webster, *Blake's Prophetic Psychology*.

5. See Bruder, *William Blake and the Daughters of Albion* and Connolly, *William Blake and the Body*. See also *William Blake and Gender* by the present writer.

6. In "Revisioning Blake's Oothoon," Harriet Kramer Linkin presents a similar, perhaps even more positive, interpretation: "While her progress towards prophecy is not constant or direct, she undergoes [...] a developmental process that results in her acquiring prophetic stature by the end of the poem" (*Blake/An Illustrated Quarterly* 23:4 [Spring 1990], 188).

7. The most detailed account of the chaining of Orc is to be found in the fifth night of *The Four Zoas*, where his father "Los nail'd him down, binding around his limbs / The accursed chain" (5: 101–2, E 341). This motif also occurs in *The First Book of Urizen*, plate 20.

8. For a substantial discussion of *The Four Zoas*, *Milton* and *Jerusalem* see my previous books *Bring Me My Arrows of Desire: Gender Utopia in Blake's The Four Zoas* and *William Blake and Gender*. These two studies deal more predominantly with issues of gender and equality than with the focus of the present chapter, sexuality.

9. The Bible reads: "For in the resurrection they neither marry, nor are given in marriage, but are as the angels of God in heaven" (Matthew 22:30).

10. This is Copy D, now in the Rosenwald Collection at the Library of Congress, Washington D.C. According to Sir Geoffrey Keynes this is the last finished by Blake of a total of four known copies (909).

11. See Michael Phillips' meticulous and significant study *William Blake: The Creation of the Songs, from Manuscript to Illuminated Printing*, 15–31 and 95–108, for a detailed documentation of Blake's working method.

12. *America*, *Europe*, *The First Book of Urizen*, *The Song of Los*, *The Book of Ahania* and *The Book of Los* fall into the category of minor prophecies; all were produced in the prolific years 1793–95. It is with good cause that Joseph Viscomi recently labelled 1795 "Blake's annus mirabilis." See "Blake's 'Annus Mirabilis': The Productions of 1795," *Blake/An Illustrated Quarterly* 41: 2 (Fall 2007), 52–83.

13. Gerald Eades Bentley Jr., ed., *William Blake's Writings*, Vol. II: Writings in Conventional Typography and in Manuscript, 1733. David Erdman, on the other hand, claims that they were most likely transcribed late in 1803 or in 1804 but, following Bentley, he also states that they might be transcribed five or more years later than this (David Erdman, *Prophet against Empire*, 1954, 3rd ed., 394n4). Geoffrey Keynes maintains that the "fair copies [were] made about 1803" (William Blake, *Complete Writings*, ed. Geoffrey Keynes, 423).

14. As is well known to Blake scholars, this is a tricky matter and the suggested year of completion among commentators traditionally varies between

1804–1808 for *Milton* and 1804–1820 for *Jerusalem*. Geoffrey Keynes proposes 1808 as the finishing year for *Milton* from the evidence of the watermarks (909), and 1818 to 1820 for *Jerusalem* by the same token (918). Blake's own printed date, however, for both poems is 1804, written on the respective frontispieces.

15. The collection acquired its name from one of its first owners, B. M. Pickering, who bought the manuscript in 1866. Before him, from 1863 to 1866, the poems were owned by Dante Gabriel Rossetti. The first owner, Fredrick Tatham, was the beneficiary of Blake's bequest. The manuscript can now be found in the Pierpont Morgan Library in New York (Keynes, 907).

16. According to Bentley, this part of the *Notebook* was written between 1801–03 (*Blake's Writings*, 1705).

17. This very rough and sketchy draft is for some reason not included in Erdman's edition of Blake's poems. However, it can be found in Keynes's edition, where it is number 9 in order on pp. 421–22.

18. The whole stanza (amended from entry 46 "The Question Answer'd") reads:

What is it men in women do
   require?
The lineaments of Gratified Desire.
What is it women do in men
   require?
The lineaments of Gratified Desire
   [E 474–75].

19. Compare Coleridge's *Ancient Mariner*:

He holds him with his glittering
   eye—
The wedding-guest stood still
And listen like a three years' child
The Mariner hath his will.

The wedding-guest sate on a stone,
He cannot choose but hear;
And thus spake on that ancient
   man,
The bright-eyed Mariner
   [17–24, in William Wordsworth and
   Samuel Taylor Coleridge, *Lyrical
   Ballads*, 115].

Notably, we here have the spellbinding glittering eye and there are obvious similarities to the old woman in "The Mental Traveller" who puts the whole poem under her spell. We can also observe the transformation of the enthralled wedding guest into a three-year-old child, reminiscent of the boy-child in Blake's poem. And, there is a guest in "The Traveller" too. As much as the Mariner "hath his will," so does the old woman. This spellbound quality makes both poems haunted travels through desert and barren lands. Its troubled spirits keep forever travelling around the world. Further strong echoes from Coleridge's poem are heard in the following stanza:

The stars, sun, Moon, all shrink away
A desart vast without a bound
And nothing left to eat or drink
And a dark desart all around
   [65–8, E 485].

The comparison is obvious: "Water, water, every where / Nor any drop to drink" (117–18, Coleridge and Wordsworth, *Lyrical Ballads*, 119).

20. For an account of the Sifting Time in Moravian history, see Moravian Brethren, *A Concise History of the Unitas Fratrum, or Church of the United Brethren, Commonly Called Moravians* and John R. Weinlick, *Count Zinzendorf*, 198.

21. To my knowledge there are not many close readings of "The Grey Monk" to be found, its complexity being a likely cause of this. Northrop

Frye devotes a couple of pages in *Fearful Symmetry* to it. According to Frye, the poem represents imaginary opposition to priests. He reads it in line with a few of its appropriate symbols, such as "the pacifist monk", "the martyr" and "the purple tyrant" (Frye, 149).

22. Both versions derive from a rather tentative draft of the poem in Blake's *Notebook* of 1800–03, which is nearly contemporary with *The Pickering Manuscript*. This draft is a mixture of the two versions consisting of nineteen stanzas in all and including frequent deletions and alterations. Also see Paley, ed., *Jerusalem*, 214, for further explication.

23. This plate has been much debated by Blake critics over the years. See for instance Morton Paley, *The Continuing City*, 113–18, and Paley, ed., *Jerusalem*, 257.

24. "[T]he first idea becomes / The hermit in a poet's metaphors" (Stevens, *Collected Poems*, 381). In his magnificent long poem "Notes Toward a Supreme fiction" Stevens describes how one, in a phenomenological way, sees the sun for the first time:

You must become an ignorant man again
And see the sun again with an ignorant eye
And see it clearly in the idea of it
[*Collected Poems*, 380].

25. I took the opportunity to consult our foremost expert, my good friend and colleague Keri Davies, who was also among the delegates, and quite enthusiastically he agreed that the illustration gives a Moravian impression.

26. See for instance Morton Paley, ed., *Jerusalem*, 152, 164–65, 193, 200, 207, 209, 217, 221, 224, 284, 292.

27. Wollstonecraft and Blake both greatly distanced themselves from conforming to the conventions of contemporary society. Both were radical idealists who visualized a utopian future where inequalities between the sexes would be erased. Hence, naturally they were seen as outcasts by their contemporaries. More remarkably, not only were they misunderstood in their own times but have continued to be so in the eyes of the common man until the present day. And most remarkably, literary critics have almost exclusively misunderstood them too.

28. As we know, Oxford Street is not a street in the city of Jerusalem; it is the female character Jerusalem who actually is in, or near to, Oxford Street of London in Blake's visionary poem. Also G. E. Bentley points this out in *The Stranger from Paradise*: "If Southey had been a little more patient, he might have remarked that Oxford Street is not in Jerusalem the city; rather the woman named Jerusalem sees 'a Gate of Precious stones and gold ... Bending across the road of Oxford Street'" (341).

Blake's Utopian "Colony"

1. See Worrall, "Thel," 42–3, for a discussion of the dates of some key publications in relation to the date of the conference. "It is possible, perhaps even likely, that the African project was discussed at the conference where Wadström played such a forward role," Worrall states (42).

2. However clear this might seem, the issue of the names of the participants is tricky and can still cause quite some confusion. Three separate documents appear to exist: the printed minutes from the meeting (a copy of which, according to David Worrall, is now in a safe in a strong room at the Swedenborg society in London ["Thel in Africa," conference paper, 1–2]), a record in the Great East Cheap Minute Book and

Robert Hindmarsh's reply to the circulating letter. An account of the latter two is given in J. R. Boyle's "Historic Notice". His explanatory note serves well to illuminate the matter:

> The "circular letter" here mentioned was not that which called the Conference, but a letter, in answer to one which had been received by the London Society from "friends at Manchester", urging Members of the New Church not to separate from the various churches with which they were already associated. The London Society's reply, signed by 77 members, was printed as an octavo pamphlet. It bears the same date as the letter calling the Conference. The reply was drawn up by Robert Hindmarsh. Nearly all the members of the London Society, male and female, signed this document, as well as several who were not members. I [J. R. Boyle] presume the statement in the Minute Book, as given above, does not mean that the whole 77 signed the Minutes of Conference, but that the 18 whose names follow signed the Minutes, and thus affirmed the principle of separation, but had not signed the reply to the letter from Manchester [ix].

3. These are the 77 people who signed the circular letter:

(SIGNED)

John Augustus Tulk. Betty Tulk. Robert Hindmarsh. Sarah Hindmarsh. Thomas Wright. George William Wright. Robert Brant. C. B. Wadstrom. Isaac Hawkins. Betty Hawkins. Robert Jackson. John Legg. Daniel Richardson. Elizabeth Richardson. Thomas Bowes. Ralph Mather. Alexander Wilderspin. Samuel Bucknall. John Hawkins. James Cruden. Manoah Sibly. Sarah Sibly. Benedict Chastanier. Joseph Jerôme Roussel. Isaac Brand. Mary Brand. John Dowling. William Attwell. William Child. John Frederic Okerblom. Elizabeth Okerblom. Samuel Hands. Charlotte Willdon. John Ball. John Sudbury. Mary Sudbury. Henrietta Edmonds. Benjamin Banks. Henry Peckitt. Robert Atchison. John Ferguson. Richard Thompson. Thomas Willdon. Mary Willdon. J. R. Needham. Robert Crane. John Willdon. James Hindmarsh. Phillis Hindmarsh. Anna Hawkins. Henry Servanté. Susanna Servanté. Henry Servanté, jun. Robert Ives. George Robinson. Hannah Robinson. William Bell. Lawrence Hill. Thomas Brant. Charles Brant. Thomas Foster. Joseph Lee. Timothy Morris. John Morley. Margaret Morley. Nanney Yandell. Samuel Bembridge. Elizabeth Bembridge. Benedict Harford. John Citizen. Elizabeth Citizen. Betty Welch. Ann Dickinson. Mary Jackson. Ann Hughes. Benjamin Bond. Samuel Smith [London: R. Hindmarsh, 1788 and London: British Library 1609.4622; 1578.3780].

4. According to Worrall, the Barthélemon couple both wrote Swedenborgian hymns, of which at least one was on an African subject. This of course strengthens the theory that the expedition to Sierra Leone was a major talking point of the gathering ("Thel," conference paper, 3).

5. This important account of the middle-passage was published only three weeks before the East Cheap conference (Worrall, "Thel," conference paper, 4). Equiano was the most prominent and probably most well known ex-slave of

that time. After being freed from the bonds of slavery he rose in standing to become quite a distinguished member of contemporary society. Hence, it is very likely that he and his book were part of the discussion at the meeting. It gives us further food for thought that Blake's acquaintance Mary Wollstonecraft had reviewed Equiano's book in *The Analytical Review*. As Helena Bergmann develops:

> Mary Wollstonecraft had read an early firsthand account from the colonies when reviewing *The Interesting Narrative of the Life of Olaudah Equiano* for *The Analytical Review*, in April 1789, taking particular note of the predicament of sexually abused female slaves (C f Fergusson 148). Her famous use of anti-slavery rhetoric to alert the public to the oppression of women in society had been appropriated by Mary Hays and other writers. As noted by Moira Fergusson in *Colonialism and Gender Relations*, *A Vindication* "contains more than eighty references" to enslavement (9). Wollstonecraft's primary use of the slavery as a concept was a striking metaphor for the subjection of women in European society, who in their "present state of civilised life, are in the same condition" (xx) as natives deprived of freedom in remote colonies [*Philosophising Females*, 17].

6. See Worrall, "Thel" conference paper, 3–4.

7. See Worrall, "Thel," 43–4.

8. See for instance Erdman, 228–48. Here he contends that

> superficially the *Visions* appears to be a debate on free love with passing allusions to the rights of man, of woman, and of beasts and to the injustices of sexual inhibition and prohibition, of life ruled by "cold floods of abstraction," and of Negro and child slavery. Yet love and slavery prove to be the two poles of the poem's axis [228].

9. Stedman's *Narrative of a five Years Expedition against the Revolted Negroes of Surinam* is one of the most important documentations of slavery and the slave-trade of the Romantic period. The *Narrative* is a firsthand account of the many experiences encountered by Captain John Gabriel Stedman while living in Surinam between 1772 and 1777. In his *Narrative*, Stedman relates several stories of the wretched state of the slaves and the horrors to which they were subjected. Stedman's *Narrative* instantly became a major literary success, was translated into a half-dozen languages and published in more than twenty-five different editions. Stedman was highly acclaimed for his insights into the slave trade and the book was adopted by the abolitionist cause. Interestingly, it took almost two centuries for a critical edition to be published. These days Stedman's *Narrative* is commonly read in university classes as an example of abolitionist literature, and it provides important reference to scholars. Blake engraved sixteen powerful images for the book between 1792 and 1794. The images depict some of the disgraceful atrocities against slaves and other natives that Stedman witnessed, including hanging, lashing and other forms of torture. Since Blake was working with *Visions of the Daughters of Albion* during this time it is highly likely that the *Narrative* became an inspiration to him and that some of the material went into it.

10. The great philanthropist and abolitionist Wadström had already been on an African expedition to Guinea set up by the Swedish attempt to establish

a combined trading and philanthropic settlement in West Africa, as promoted by King Gustav III. Wadström was deeply shocked and disgusted by the conditions and the brutality of the slave trade, which he described in *Observations on the Slave Trade, and a Description of some part of the Coast of Guinea* from 1789.

11. When examining the original of the painting, now in the Nordiska Museet in Stockholm, there are two immediately striking things. One is the extreme vividness of the motif of the painting and the presence of the two characters becomes a nearly physical in-the-room experience. The other is the strong pedagogical emphasis of the situation with the benevolent and idealistic Wadström in focus, eager to teach the black boy.

12. Alarmingly weak on the connections between Swedenborg, Blake and sexuality, Robert Rix incorrectly half-dismisses this crucial link: "Critics have pointed to the possible influence of Swedenborg's sexual theories on Blake's *The Four Zoas* (begun c. 1796) and the late poetry." Rix claims that this was a component already in the early poems (99). Remarkably, on the next page he goes on to inform us that Swedenborg proposed that men and women go on to exist after death in a heavenly version of the mundane world, for one thing still enjoying sex. Surely, this is also a major idea in Blake's three long epic prophecies. Rix completely fails to see this connection and only mentions a couple of Blake's illustrations as examples of his adaptation of this important concept in Swedenborg (100).

13. See my *William Blake and Gender*, 49–50, for a more detailed discussion of Pantisocracy.

14. See also Ogude, "Swedenborg and Blake's Little Black Boy" and Paley, "A New Heaven is Begun."

15. This German phrase should roughly be translated as "a female community will come into being (in the future)."

16. We know that by that time Blake had annotated *Heaven and Hell, Divine Love and Divine Wisdom* and *Divine Providence*. According to Erdman, he had also read *Apocalypse Revealed* (142–43). He further suggests that "Blake may have been reading in Swedenborg as early as 1787, the date of the pamphlet he cites as 'Worlds in Universe' (*Earths in the Universe*)." Moreover, Erdman writes that Blake in fact owned the 1784 edition of *Heaven and Hell* (139).

17. It is not unlikely that Blake found inspiration for this double-edged critical image of women as slaves from his acquaintance Mary Wollstonecraft, whom he met at Joseph Johnson's bookshop and collaborated with at that time. And as pointed out before, there are obvious connections between *Visions* and *Vindication of the Rights of Woman*. In her famous treatise Wollstonecraft uses slavery as a compelling metaphor for patriarchal enchainment of women. In *Philosophising Females* Helena Bergmann elaborates on Wollstonecraft's notion of female slaves:

> Mary Wollstonecraft's tract [*Vindication*] abounds in other provocatively demeaning descriptions of women not only as slaves, but as "gentle, domestic brutes" (23), who have been prevented from developing their intellectual resources. When no efforts are made to cast off the "hereditary trappings" (26), men remain the "tyrants" and women their "slaves" (29), confining one of the sexes to a childlike status of ignorance and enfeeblement. The slavery theme is reiterated in recurring images of

physical entrapment or bondage, the most portentous one being in "the adamantine chain of destiny" (40). Wollstonecraft's perspective was that of a superior, enlightened woman, with the ambition to incite her fellow sisters to take action against repressed anger and being forced to "bite the bridle" of discontent [40].

18. See Rix, 146–54.
19. Anti-slavery discourse was put to pertinent use by Wollstonecraft in order to expose the inequalities between the sexes. Yet, her rhetoric has been criticized as springing from a European middle class perspective. Ostracizing female vanity, she asserts that an "immoderate fondness for dress, for pleasure, and for sway, are the passions of savages; the passions that occupy those savage beings who have not yet extended the dominion of the mind" (*Vindication*, 207–208). Her primary concern was dogmatic: women must in every way be taught to become "rational creatures" (41) and raise themselves from the status of "brute" or "slave" (Bergmann, "Brutes, Bridles and Chains," 5.)

Conclusion

1. See "Blake and the 1790s Plebeian Radical Culture" in Clark and Worrall, *Blake in the Nineties*, 194–211.
2. See "The Will of Henry Banes, Landlord of 3 Fountain Court, Strand, the Last Residence of William and Catherine Blake," *Blake/An Illustrated Quarterly* 39: 2 (2005), 78–99.
3. See particularly Michael Phillips, *The Creation of the Songs from Manuscript to Illuminated Printing*.
4. See Mei-Ying Sung, *William Blake and the Art of Engraving*.

Bibliography

Works by William Blake

Blake, William. *Blake's "America: A Prophecy" and "Europe: A Prophecy" Facsimile Reproductions of Two Illuminated Books.* New York: Dover, 1983.

———. *The Complete Poetry and Prose.* Ed. David V. Erdman, commentary Harold Bloom. New York: Anchor-Doubleday, 1988.

———. *Complete Writings.* Ed. Geoffrey Keynes. (1957). Oxford: Oxford University Press, 1985.

———. *The Early Illuminated Books.* Vol. 3. (*All Religions are One, There is no Natural Religion, The Book of Thel, The Marriage of Heaven and Hell, Visions of the Daughters of Albion*). Ed. Morris Eaves, Robert N. Essick, and Joseph Viscomi. London: Tate Gallery, 1993.

———. *The First Book of Urizen.* In *The Urizen Books.*

———. *The Four Zoas. A Photographic Facsimile of the Manuscript with Commentary on the Illuminations.* Ed. and commentary Cettina Tramontano Magno and David V. Erdman. London and Toronto: Associated University Press, 1987.

———. *The Four Zoas. The Torments in Love and Jealousy in the Death and Judgment of Albion the Ancient Man.* Ed. Landon Dowdey. Chicago: The Swallow Press, 1983.

———. *The Four Zoas. Vala; or, The Four Zoas. A Facsimile of the Manuscript, a Transcript of the Poem, and a Study of its Growth and Significance.* Ed. G. E. Bentley, Jr. Oxford: Clarendon Press, 1963.

———. *Jerusalem.* Vol. 1. Ed. Morton D. Paley. London: Tate Gallery, 1993.

———. *The Marriage of Heaven and Hell.* Commentary Geoffrey Keynes. Oxford: Oxford University Press, 1986.

———. *Milton.* Vol. 5. Ed. Robert N. Essick and Joseph Viscomi. London: Tate Gallery, 1993.

———. *Songs of Experience.* New York: Dover, 1984.

———. *Songs of Innocence.* New York: Dover, 1971.

———. *The Urizen Books.* Vol. 6. (*The First Book of Urizen, The Book of Ahania, The Book of Los*) Ed. David Worrall. London: Tate Gallery, 1995.

———. *Visions of the Daughters of Albion.* In *The Early Illuminated Books.*

Other Works

Abrams, Lynn. *The Making of Modern Woman: Europe 1789–1918.* London: Pearson Education, 2002.

Andrews, Stuart. *Unitarian Radicalism: Political Rhetoric, 1770–1814.* Basingstoke and New York: Palgrave MacMillan, 2003.

Ankarsjö, Magnus. *Bring Me My Arrows of Desire: Gender Utopia in Blake's The Four Zoas.* Göteborg: Acta Universitatis Gothoburgensis, 2004.

_____. *William Blake and Gender*. Jefferson, NC: McFarland, 2006.

Atwood, Craig. *Community of the Cross*. University Park: Pennsylvania State University Press, 2004.

_____. "Sleeping in the Arms of Christ." *Journal of the History of Sexuality*, vol. 8 (1977), 25–51.

Bentley, G. E. Jr. *Blake Records*. 2nd ed. New Haven and London: Yale University Press, 2004.

_____. *The Stranger from Paradise: A Biography of William Blake*. New Haven and London: Yale University Press, 2001.

_____, ed. *William Blake's Writings*, Vol. II: Writings in Conventional Typography and in Manuscript. Oxford: Oxford University Press, 1978.

Bergmann, Helena. "Brutes, Bridles and Chains: On the Debatable Domain of Slavery in the Writings of Wollstonecraft, Hays and Hamilton." Unpublished conference paper, presented at BARS "Debatable Lands" at Newcastle upon Tyne July 29, 2005.

_____. *Philosophising Females*. Lampeter: Edwin Mellen Press, 2009.

The Holy Bible. The Authorized King James Version, 1611. Cambridge: Cambridge University Press, 2001.

Bogen, Nancy. "The Problem of William Blake's Early Religion." *The Personalist* 49 (1968).

Boyle, J. R. "Historic Notice of the Early Conferences." In *Minutes of the First Seven Sessions of the General Conference of the New Church signified by the New Jerusalem in the Revelation, together with those of other contemporary assemblies of a similar character reprinted from the original editions*. London: James Spiers, 1885, ix-xl.

Brody, Miriam. Introduction to *A Vindication of the Rights of Woman*. London: Penguin, 1992, 7–72.

Brown, K.D. *A Social History of the Nonconformist Ministry in England and Wales 1800–1930*. Oxford: Clarendon Press, 1988.

Bruce, Jack. *Travels to Discover the Source of the Nile, in Egypt, Arabia, Abyssinia, and Nubia*. Dublin: Zachariah Jackson, 1790.

Bruder, Helen. "Blake and Gender Studies." In *Palgrave Advances in Blake Studies*, ed. Nicholas Williams, 132–66.

_____. *William Blake and the Daughters of Albion*. Basingstoke: Macmillan, 1997.

_____, ed. *Women Reading William Blake*. Basingstoke: Palgrave, 2007.

Chevalier, Tracey. *Burning Bright*. London: Harper Collins, 2007.

Clark, Steve. Review of Bruder, *William Blake and the Daughters of Albion*. TLS Dec. 5, 1997. Accessed May 14, 2008: <http://tls.timesonline.co.uk/article/0,,25363-1955134_1,00.html>.

Clark, Steve, and David Worrall, eds. *Blake in the Nineties*. Basingstoke: MacMillan, 1999.

_____, and _____. *Blake, Nation and Empire*. Basingstoke and New York: Palgrave Macmillan, 2006.

Clark, Steve, and Masashi Suzuki, eds. *The Reception of Blake in the Orient*. London and New York: Continuum, 2006.

Coleridge, Samuel Taylor. "The Rhyme of the Ancient Mariner." In *Coleridge and William Wordsworth, Lyrical Ballads*, 1798. Plymouth: Northcote House, 1987.

A Collection of Hymns by Several Authors. With Several Translation from the German Hymn-book of Ancient Morvian Brethren. For the Use of Several Religious Societies. London: Printed for James Hutton, 1741.

A Collection of Hymns, with Several Translations from the Hymn-Book of the Moravian Brethren. 2nd ed. London: 1743.

Colley, Linda. *Britons: Forging the Nation, 1707–1837*. New Haven: Yale University Press, 1992.

Connolly, Tristanne. *William Blake and the Body*. Basingstoke and New York: Palgrave MacMillan, 2002.

Davies, Keri. "Blake and the Moravians." Unpublished conference paper. 2007.

———. "The Lost Moravian History of William Blake's Family: Snapshots from the Archive." *Blackwell's Literature Compass*, 1–31. March 20, 2009 <http://blackwell-compass.com/subject/literature/>.

———. "Mrs Bliss: A Blake Collector of 1794." In Clark and Worrall, eds., *Blake in the Nineties*. Basingstoke: Macmillan, 1999, 212–30.

———. Review of *The Stranger from Paradise: A Biography of William Blake*, by G. E. Bentley, Jr. *The Blake Journal* 7 (2002), 62–70.

———. *William Blake in Contexts: Family, Friendships, and Some Intellectual Microcultures of Eighteenth- and Nineteenth-Century England*. Unpub. diss. St. Mary's College, Strawberry Hill, Twickenham, 2003.

———. "William Blake's Mother: a New Identification." *Blake/An Illustrated Quarterly*, 33: 2 (Fall 1999), 36–50.

———. "The Winepress of Love: Dissent, Antinomianism, and William Blake's Moravian Inheritance." Unpub. conference paper. Blake at 250, July-Aug. 2007, The University of York.

Davies, Keri, and Marsha Keith Schuchard. "Recovering the Lost Moravian History of William Blake's Family." *Blake/An Illustrated Quarterly* 38.1 (Summer 2004), 36–43.

Erdman, David V. *Blake: Prophet Against Empire*. Princeton, NJ: Princeton University Press, 1969.

Fergusson, Moira. *Colonialism and Gender Relations from Mary Wollstonecraft to Jamaica Kincaid: East Caribbean Connections*. New York: Columbia University Press, 1993.

Frye, Northrop. *Fearful Symmetry: A Study of William Blake*. Princeton: Princeton University Press, 1947.

Gilchrist, Alexander. *The Life of William Blake*, 1863. Ed. Ruthven Todd. London: J. M. Dent & Sons, 1982.

Gleadle, Kathryn. *British Women in the Nineteenth Century*. Basingstoke: Palgrave, 2001.

Godwin, William. *Memoirs of the Author of A Vindication of the Rights of Woman*, 1798. Ed. Clemit, Pamela, and Gina Luria Walker. Peterborough, Ont.: Broadview Press, 2001.

Gott, Dorothy. *The Midnight Cry, "Behold, the Bridegroom Comes!" or, An Order from God to Get your Lamps Lighted*. London: 1788.

Hagen F. F. *Old Landmarks*. Bethlehem, PA: Hagen, 1886.

Hamilton, Joseph. *Johnson's Dictionary of the English Language in Miniature*. 8th ed. London, 1797.

Hassé, E. R. *The Moravians*. London: National Council of Evangelical Free Churches in London, 1911.

Hays, Mary. *The Memoirs of Emma Courtney*. (1796). London: Pandora Press, 1987.

Hessayon, Ariel. "Jacob Boehme, Emanuel Swedenborg and their Readers." In *The Arms of Morpheus — Essays on Swedenborg and Mysticism, Journal of the Swedenborg Society* 2007, 17–56.

Hindmarsh, Robert. *Minutes of a General Conference of the Members of the New Church, Signified by the New Jerusalem in the Revelation*. London: R. Hindmarsh, 1789.

Hobson, Christopher. *Blake and Homosexuality*. Basingstoke: Palgrave MacMillan, 2000.

Johnson, Mary Lynn. "Feminist Approaches to Teaching Songs." In *Ap-

proaches to Teaching Blake's Songs, ed. Robert F. Gleckner. New York: Modern Language Association, 1989, 57–66.

Juster, Susan. *Doomsayers: Anglo-American Prophecies in the Age of Revolution*. University of Pennsylvania Press, 2003.

Keynes, Geoffrey. "Notes." In William Blake, *Complete Writings*, ed. Geoffrey Keynes. Oxford: Oxford University Press, 1985. 883–928.

Lincoln, Andrew. "Blake and the History of Radicalism." In *Palgrave Advances in William Blake Studies*, ed. Nicholas Williams, 214- 234.

Linkin, Harriet Kramer. "Revisioning Blake's Oothoon." *Blake/An Illustrated Quarterly* 23:4 (Spring 1990), 184–194.

Madan, Martin. *Thelyphthora; Or, A Treatise on Female Ruin, in its Causes, Effects, Consequences, Prevention, and Remedy; Considered on the Basis of Divine Law*. London: J. Podsley, 1780.

McCalmann, Ian, ed. *An Oxford Companion to the Romantic Age: British Culture 1776–1832*. Oxford: Oxford University Press, 1999.

Mee, Jon. *Dangerous Enthusiasm: William Blake and the Culture of Radicalism in the 1790s*. Oxford: Clarendon Press, 1992.

———. *Romanticism, Enthusiasm, and Regulation: Poetics and the Policing of Culture in the Romantic Period*. Oxford: Oxford University Press, 2003.

Mellor, Anne K. "Blake's Portrayal of Women." *Blake/An Illustrated Quarterly* Winter (1982–83), 148–55.

Moravian Brethren. *A Concise History of the Unitas Fratrum, or Church of the United Brethren, Commonly Called Moravians*. London: Mallalieu & Co., 1862.

Moravian Church Library and Archive. AB38. Minutes of Saturday Conferences, 1744–5. Conference, On Saturday, May 4, 15, 1745.

———. "MORAVIANS NOT DISSENTERS." Letter to the editor of the *Manchester Courier*, *Manchester Courier* May 29, 1872.

Ogude, S. E. "Swedenborg and Blake's 'Little Black Boy.'" *Asemka* 4 (1976), 85_96.

Ostriker, Alicia. "Desire Gratified and Ungratified: William Blake and Sexuality." *Blake/An Illustrated Quarterly* Winter (1982–83), 156–65.

Paley, Morton. *The Continuing City*. Oxford: Oxford University Press, 1983.

———. "'A New Heaven Is Begun': Blake and Swedenborgianism." *Blake/An Illustrated Quarterly* 12 (2), 64–90.

———. *The Traveller in the Evening: The Last Works of William Blake*. Oxford: Oxford University Press, 2003.

———, ed. *Jerusalem*. Blake's Illuminated Books, vol. 1. London: Tate Gallery, 1993.

Phillips, Michael. *William Blake: The Creation of the Songs from Manuscript to Illuminated Printing*. London: British Library, 2000.

Podmore, Colin. *The Fetter Lane Moravian Congregation, London 1742–1992*. London: Fetter Lane Moravian Congregation, 1992.

———. *The Moravian Church in England, 1728_1760*. Oxford: Clarendon Press, 1998.

Poovey, Mary. *The Proper Lady and the Woman Writer: Ideology as Style in the Works of Mary Wollstonecraft, Mary Shelley and Jane Austen*. Chicago and London: University of Chicago Press, 1984.

Prickett, Stephen, and Christopher Strathman. "Blake and the Bible." In *Palgrave Advances in Blake Studies*, ed. Nicholas Williams, 109–131.

Priestley, Joseph. *Discourses on the Evidence of Revealed Religion.* London: Joseph Johnson, 1794.

———. *Discourses.* Vol. 3. London and Birmingham: Multiple publishers, 1790–96.

———. *Letters to The Members of the New Jerusalem Church, formed by Baron Swedenborg.* Birmingham: J. Thompson, 1791.

———. "Reflections on Death. A Sermon, on occasion of the Death of The Rev. Robert Robertson, of Cambridge." Birmingham: J. Belcher, 1790. In Joseph Priestley. *Discourses,* Vol. 3.

Rimius, Henry. *A Candid Narrative of the Rise and Progress of the Herrnhuters: Commonly Call'd Moravians or Unitas Fratrum.* London: A. Linde, 1753.

Rix, Robert. *William Blake and the Cultures of Radical Christianity.* Aldershot and Burlington, VT: Ashgate, 2007.

Robinson, Henry Crabb. *On Books and their Writers.* Vol. 1. Ed. Edith J. Morley. London: J.M. Dent and Sons, 1938.

———. "William Blake, Künstler, Dichter und religiöser Schwärmer." *Vaterländisches Museum 1* (1811), rpt. in *Blake Records 2,* 583.

Schorer, Mark. *William Blake: The Politics of Vision.* New York: Henry Holt & Co., 1946.

Schuchard, Marsha Keith. *Why Mrs Blake Cried: William Blake and the Sexual Basis of Spiritual Vision.* London: Century, 2006.

———. "The 'Secret' and the 'Gift': Recovering the Suppressed Religious Heritage of William Blake and Hilda Doolittle. In Bruder, *Women Reading Blake,* 209–18.

Spilling, James. "Blake the Visionary." *New Church Magazine,* VI (1887).

Southey, Robert. *The Doctor.* London: 1847.

Stead, Geoffrey. *The Moravian Settlement at Fulneck, 1742–1790.* Leeds: Thoresby Society, 1999.

Stedman, John Gabriel. *A Narrative of a five years' expedition, against the Revolted Negroes of Surinam from the year 1772 to 1777, elucidating the History of that Country and Describing its Productions.* London: Joseph Johnson, 1796.

Stevens, Wallace. "Notes Toward a Supreme Fiction." From *Transport to Summer* in *Collected Poems.* London and Boston: Faber and Faber, 1987, 380–408.

Sung, Mei-Ying. *William Blake and the Art of Engraving.* London: Pickering & Chatto, 2009.

Swedenborg, Emanuel. *The Delights of Wisdom concerning Conjugial Love, after which follows The Pleasures of Insanity concerning Scortatory Love,* 1768. London: Swedenborg Society, 1953.

———. *The Generative Organs Considered Anatomically, Physically and Philosophically.* Trans J. J. Garth Wilkinson. London: William Newberry, 1852.

———. *Heaven and Hell.* (1758). London: Swedenborg Society, 1885.

Taylor, Barbara. *Mary Wollstonecraft and the Feminist Imagination.* Cambridge: Cambridge University Press, 2003.

Thompson, E. P. *Witness Against the Beast: William Blake and the Moral Law.* Cambridge: Cambridge University Press, 1993.

Thorild, Thomas. *True Heavenly Religion Restored.* London: R. Hindmarsh, 1790.

Tomalin, Claire. *Shelley and his World,* 1980. London: Penguin, 1992.

United Brethren of Christ. *A Collection of Hymns of the Children of God in all Ages, from the Beginning till Now.* London, 1754.

Viscomi, Joe. "Blake's 'Annus Mirabilis': The Productions of 1795." *Blake/An Illustrated Quarterly* 41 (2), 52–83.

Wadström, Carl Bernard. *Observations on the Slave Trade, and a Description of some part of the Coast of Guinea, during a Voyage Made in 1787, and 1788*. London: J. Phillips, 1789.

———. *Plan for a Free Community upon the Coast of Africa*. London: R. Hindmarsh, 1789.

Watts, Ruth. *Gender, Power and the Unitarians in England 1760–1860*. London: Longman, 1998.

Webster, Brenda. *Blake's Prophetic Psychology*. London: Macmillan, 1983.

Weinlick, John R. *Count Zinzendorf*. New York and Nashville: Abingdon Press, 1956.

White, Daniel. *Early Romanticism and Religious Dissent*. Cambridge and New York: Cambridge University Press, 2006.

Whitehead, Angus. "The Will of Henry Banes, Landlord of 3 Fountain Court, Strand, the Last Residence of William and Catherine Blake." *Blake/An Illustrated Quarterly* 39: 2 (2005), 78–99.

Whittaker, Jason. "Mental Fight, Corporeal War, and Righteous Dub: The Struggle for Jerusalem in Popular Music." Unpublished conference paper, presented at "Blake and Conflict" at The University of Oxford September 22–23, 2006.

———, and Shirley Dent. *Radical Blake: Influence and Afterlife from 1827*. Basingstoke and New York: Palgrave and Macmillan, 2002.

Williams Nicholas, ed. *Palgrave Advances in Blake Studies*. Basingstoke and New York: Palgrave Macmillan, 2006.

Wollstonecraft, Mary. *A Vindication of the Rights of Woman*. (1792). London: Dent, 1974.

———. *Mary, or, the Wrongs of Woman. The Wrongs of Woman*. (1798). In *Mary and The Wrongs of Woman*. Oxford and New York: Oxford University Press, 1987, 71–204.

Wood, Marcus. *Slavery, Empathy and Pornogaphy*. Oxford: Oxford University Press, 2002.

Wordsworth, William, and Samuel Taylor Coleridge. *Lyrical Ballads*. (1798). Plymouth: Northcote House, 1987.

Worrall, David. "Blake and the 1790s Plebeian Culture." In *Blake in the Nineties*, ed. Steve Clark and David Worrall, 194–211.

———. "Thel in Africa." In *Blake, Nation and Empire*, ed. Steve Clark and David Worrall, 40–62.

———. "Thel in Africa: William Blake and the Post-colonial, Post-Swedenborgian Female Subject." In *The Reception of Blake in the Orient*, 17–28.

———. "Thel in Africa." Unpublished conference paper, presented at "Blake in the Orient" at Kyoto University November 29–30, 2003.

Index

abolition 121, 123, 125, 134, 149
Act of Toleration (1689) 12, 45
Act of Toleration (1742) 37
Act of Uniformity (1662) 12, 45
Act of Unitas Fratrum 37–8
Africa 27–8, 91, 121–3, 125, 127, 130, 133, 138, 147–50
Ahania 91–3, 96
Albion 57, 61–5, 94–5, 99, 131; daughters of 63, 130–1
America 34–5, 37, 45, 119, 130–1
America: A Prophecy 88–9, 91, 131–3, 145
anecdote 79–80, 113–4, 116, 136; *see also* critical fallacies
angels 22–4, 52–4, 66, 73, 76–7, 109, 112, 115–6, 130, 145
Anglicanism 12, 33
antinomianism 11–12, 26, 67, 139; *see also* denominationalism; nonconformity
apocalypse 19, 25, 27, 43, 56–64, 90, 93, 95–9, 127, 131–2, 144, 150
Apocrypha 27, 126–7
Arians 15
Armitage (Harmitage/Hermitage), Thomas 5–6, 14, 32, 137

Bentley, G.E., Jr. 48, 100, 113–14, 116–17, 144–7
Bergmann, Helena 149–51
Beulah 59–60, 114, 135
Bible 14, 16, 19, 21, 24–5, 27–8, 34, 53, 56, 50–62, 64–7, 76, 94, 97, 116, 121, 126–7, 145
biography 5–6, 18, 35, 48, 62, 70, 79, 83, 85, 100, 103, 113, 116–17
bischöflischer Kirche 48–9; *see also* Church of England; Episcopal Church; Staatskirche; state church
Blake, Catherine (mother) 5–8, 14, 32–3, 46, 107, 136–7
Blake, Catherine (wife) 27, 46, 121, 135, 138, 151
Blake, James (father) 5, 8, 14, 137, 142
Blake, John (uncle) 6, 32

Blake studies 1–4, 6–7, 9, 33, 48, 70, 122, 136–7, 141
blood 26, 41–2, 44, 55, 62, 105, 108–10, 144; *see also* side-wound; wound
Bohemia 36, 40
Böhler, Peter 36–7
The Book of Ahania 91–2, 134, 139, 145
Book of Enoch 27, 126
The Book of Los 92, 134, 139, 145
The Book of Thel 71–4, 122–5, 130
Brockmer, John Paul 31
Bromion 86–8, 130
brotherhood 20, 25, 35, 38, 41, 43, 56, 65, 111, 123
Bruce, Jack 27, 126
Bruder, Helen 2–4, 71, 73, 77, 80, 87–8, 141, 145

Chastanier, Benedict 120, 148
Chevalier, Tracey 80
Christ *see* Jesus
Christianity 4, 6–7, 11–12, 15, 20–2, 38, 41, 43, 48, 53, 55, 65–6, 68, 99, 102, 109–12, 116, 123, 137, 142, 144
Church of England 5–6, 11–14, 26, 37–8, 45, 48, 139; *see also* bischöflischer Kirche; Episcopal Church; Staatskirche; state church
Coleridge, Samuel Taylor 16, 31, 105, 125–6, 129, 146
colony 31, 33, 35, 40, 82, 118, 123–26, 130, 147
community 15, 25, 29–31, 35, 39–41, 48–9, 95, 118, 123, 125–7, 144, 150; *see also* Gemeinde
concubinage 30
conference 17–18, 21, 23, 27, 28, 31, 37, 40, 46–50, 86, 111, 118–24, 128–9, 130, 134–5, 137–9, 144–5, 147–9
conjugal 29, 33, 39, 82, 121, 123–7
conjugal love 29–30, 32–3, 39, 121, 125, 127, 134
Connolly, Tristanne 2, 4, 80, 141, 145
conservativatism 1–2, 22–3, 26, 30, 42, 50, 108, 142–3

159

convention *see* conference
creation myth 66, 91–2, 140
critical fallacies 7–8, 136; *see also* anecdotes
"The Crystal Cabinet" 107, 114–15

Damon, S. Foster 7
Davies, Keri 4–8, 14, 31, 38, 44–6, 48–9, 55, 70, 107, 136–8, 141–4, 147
Delegate (at Great East Cheap conference) 40, 47, 86, 111, 119, 121, 147; *see also* subscriber
denominationalism 12, 15, 20, 31, 37, 139, 142; *see also* antinomianism; nonconformity
desire 2, 28–9, 39, 51–2, 74–6, 81–4, 92, 94, 96, 104, 132, 145–6
dissent 6–7, 11–12, 14, 18–20, 22, 24, 33, 37–8, 41, 45–6, 48–9, 136, 142–4

Eden 52, 64, 94, 115
education 16–17, 20, 28, 40, 142
ejaculation 52, 76, 96, 115
Eliot, T. S. 7
emanation 61, 64, 66, 94–9, 101
Enion 57, 93, 96
Enitharmon 56–8, 61, 89–90, 93–4, 96–7, 99
Enlightenment, the 18, 27–8, 38
enthusiasm 12–13, 22, 141–2
epic 41, 43, 56, 64, 78, 81, 89–90, 93–5, 97, 99–100, 102, 111, 113, 117–18, 133–5, 150
Episcopal Church 38, 144; *see also* bischöflisher Kirche; Church of England; Staatskirche; state church
Equiano 120, 122, 148–9
Erdman, David V. 67, 142, 144–6, 149–50
eroticism 4, 27, 39, 41, 44, 79, 87, 94
Eternity 57–60, 63–6, 72, 84, 89–94, 96–7, 99, 102, 107, 124, 130, 133
Europe 89–91, 133, 145
Evangelical Revival 13, 37–8, 40, 45
"The Everlasting Gospel" 65–9
Experience 71–2

fall (of man) 45, 58–9, 68–9, 88–90, 92–6
Felpham 62, 100, 103, 116
female will 3, 66
femininity 13, 44, 77
feminism 1–3, 5–6, 8, 13, 16–7, 26, 30, 43, 79–80, 87, 89, 127
feminist position 2–4
Fetter Lane 5, 7, 31, 35–7, 42, 46, 143
The First Book of Urizen 133, 145
Flaxman, Ann "Nancy" 69
Flaxman, John 27, 69

forgiveness of sins 20, 25, 41, 53, 56, 64–5, 67–9, 101–2, 110–11
four zoas 62–4, 95–6, 98
The Four Zoas 39, 57–65, 78, 81, 93–101, 117, 132, 134–5, 144–5, 150
free love 39, 78–80, 90, 102, 112, 149
The French Revolution 15, 132–3
Fuseli, Henry 78–9, 116

Gemeinde 48–9; *see also* community
gender 1–6, 16–17, 25, 44, 53–6, 63, 71, 76–7, 80–1, 87–9, 91, 93–4, 98–9, 122, 129, 134, 141–3, 145, 149–50; equality 29, 43, 71, 81, 93, 97–8, 125–9, 131, 145
generation 56
genitals 32–3, 39, 41, 44, 52, 71, 74, 87, 92, 99, 109, 111, 114, 136, 144
Gilchrist, Alexander 18
Godwin, William 14, 18, 78–9
Golgonooza 99
Gott, Dorothy 119–21, 138
(Great) East Cheap 11, 21, 23, 25, 28, 40, 46, 50, 86, 118, 120, 122, 128–30, 134, 137–9, 147–8
"The Grey Monk" 42–3, 107–11, 146–7
Gustav III, King 29, 150

Harmitage, Thomas *see* Armitage, Thomas
Hayley, William 100, 117
Hays, Mary 3, 16–18, 149
Hermitage, Thomas *see* Armitage, Thomas
Herrnhut 35–6, 40
Hindmarsh, Robert 22–3, 118, 142–4, 147–8
Hobson, Christopher 4, 141
holism 90
humanism 4, 20, 49, 140
Hussites 36
hymn 39–41, 43–4, 54–5, 86, 144, 148

"I Saw a Chapel All of Gold" 51–2, 75, 143
illuminated writing 49–50, 98, 100, 107, 117, 132–3, 139, 145, 151
imagination 8, 18, 27, 39, 44, 66, 76, 94
individualism 16, 19, 25
innocence 58–9, 62, 71–3, 88, 90, 104

jealousy 53, 74, 81–2, 86–8, 91, 94, 96, 101
Jerusalem (character) 57–8, 62, 64, 96, 99, 147
Jerusalem (city) 25, 58, 62, 96, 113, 128, 145, 147
Jerusalem (poem) 20, 25–6, 33, 41, 43, 53, 61–5, 67–8, 93–5, 97–102, 107, 109–11, 113, 117, 128, 131–2, 134–5, 145–7

Index

Jesus 13, 19–20, 25, 26, 35, 38–44, 53, 55–9, 62, 64, 66–7, 93, 96, 105–6, 108–11, 142–3
Johnson, Joseph 8, 14–5, 18, 20, 133, 150

Keats, John 105–6
Keynes, Geoffrey 67, 75, 77–8, 81, 100, 145–6

lamb 54–5, 57–60, 73, 92
"The Little Black Boy" 28, 122–3, 150
London 5–6, 16, 22, 27–8, 31, 35–7, 42, 45, 118, 120, 123, 142–4, 147–8
Los 57–8, 61, 65, 92–3, 96–7, 99, 133, 145
love 16, 25, 29–30, 32–3, 39, 41, 51–4, 57, 65, 70, 74–9, 81–8, 90–96, 101–3, 106–7, 111–13, 115–17, 123, 125–7, 130, 139–40, 144, 149
love-feast 43–4
Luvah 59–60, 63, 96, 135

Madan, Martin 122
madness 31, 112–14, 116
marriage 5, 29, 32, 39–40, 74, 82, 84, 94, 100, 102–4, 115, 123–4, 127, 131–2, 134, 145
The Marriage of Heaven and Hell 18, 23–4, 33, 43, 47–8, 50–1, 67, 76–7, 111, 129, 143
masonry 119–20, 142
masturbation 82
materialism 16
Matthew 94, 145
meeting *see* conference
Mellor, Anne 2, 80, 145
The Memoirs of Emma Courtney 17
"The Mental Traveller" 104–6, 146
Methodism 37–8, 142
millennium 21, 23, 43
Milton (character) 61, 98
Milton (poem) 26, 47, 61–2, 89–90, 93–5, 97–100, 103, 117, 128, 134–5, 145–6
Milton, John (poet) 135
minutes (of Great East Cheap meeting) 31, 118, 144, 147–8
misogyny 2–3, 80, 85; *see also* sexist
missionary 34–8, 40, 124, 126–7
Moravian Brethren 34–8, 44, 144; *see also* Unitas Fratrum
Moravian Church Archive 5; *see also* Muswell Hill
Moravianism 5–8, 11–14, 18, 20, 26, 31–3, 34–45, 46, 48–9, 51, 53–60, 62, 65, 67, 69–70, 73, 75, 78, 82, 85–8, 93, 99, 102, 105, 107–12, 124, 126, 129, 136–7, 139, 141–3, 146–7

Muggletonian/-ism 7–8, 11, 13–14, 18, 142
Muir, William 5
Muswell Hill 5–6; *see also* Moravian Church Archive
mythology 20, 45, 48, 56, 78, 81, 89–90, 93, 95, 114–15, 117, 133–4

Natural/Sexual Religion 19, 49, 127
negation 53, 57, 60, 64, 90, 92, 94, 100, 103, 110
new discoveries 1, 5–8, 14, 31, 33, 48, 70, 107, 111, 136, 139
New Jerusalem Church 21, 23, 26–8, 46, 119, 125, 143
nonconformity 8, 11, 14, 142; *see also* antinomianism; denominationalism
Nordenskjöld, August 28–9, 119–21, 123, 127, 143
Nordenskjöld, Carl-Fredric 28
Notebook 8, 50–1, 53–4, 66, 74–5, 77, 79, 81–2, 84–6, 99–100, 103–4, 117, 143, 146–7
Nottinghamshire 5, 37
nudity 33, 39, 52, 59, 74, 80, 117, 120, 132, 136, 144; *see also* naked

Old Dissent 12
Ololon 61, 95, 98, 135
Oothoon 71–2, 78, 80, 86–91, 130, 134, 145
Ostriker, Alicia 2, 80, 145

Paley, Morton 24, 27, 47, 50, 62, 65, 67, 147, 150
Panah, Peter 27–8, 122–3
Pantisocracy 125, 150
Paradise 48, 58, 64, 68–9, 79, 147
passion 17, 39, 43, 63, 75, 112, 151
patriarchal tradition 2; *see also* misogyny; sexism
patriarchy 2, 6, 30, 47, 73, 87, 122, 125–6, 128, 130, 150
penis 39, 52, 73, 76, 83, 115, 144
Pennsylvania 35, 125–6
The Pickering Manuscript 8, 42–3, 85, 99–100, 103–4, 106–7, 109, 112, 115–17, 146–7
Presbyterianism 12, 15, 142
Priestley, Joseph 14–15, 17–22, 24, 126, 142
prophecy 19–20, 23, 25, 43, 45, 47, 56, 61, 71, 73, 80–1, 83, 88–9, 94–5, 99–102, 104, 110, 118, 120–1, 130–4, 138, 145, 150
Protestantism 11, 35, 38, 40, 45, 142
publishing/printing 8, 14–15, 20, 24, 28, 40, 43, 132–3, 138–9, 145, 151

radical Christianity 7, 11, 137
radicalism 2–4, 6–8, 11, 14–17, 19–23, 27,

30, 32, 41, 45–6, 48–9, 79–81, 88, 109, 112–13, 120–1, 124–5, 132–3, 136–7, 139, 141–4, 147, 151
rational dissent 18
reason 18–9, 22–3, 39, 77
reunion 32, 43, 61–2, 64, 66, 95, 97–8, 134
revolution 16, 23, 38, 40, 45–6, 63, 78–9, 88, 105, 131, 132, 141–2; American 45, 131; French 16, 23, 40, 45–6, 132, 142
Rix, Robert 7, 11–13, 21, 23, 25–6, 32, 43, 45–8, 119–20, 123, 128, 132–3, 137, 142–4, 150–1
Robinson, Henry Crabb 16, 48–9, 113, 116, 127
Romanticism 1, 11–13, 78–9, 149
Rousseau, Jean-Jacques 17, 110, 142

St. Paul's Churchyard 18
Saxony 34, 36
Schorer, Mark 5, 48
Schuchard, Marsha Keith 5–8, 31–2, 39, 42, 75, 107, 136, 141, 143
serpent 52, 54, 64, 76, 132
sexism 1–2, 73, 80, 136; *see also* misogyny
sexual/gender politics 3, 23, 26, 29, 58, 70, 80, 99, 124, 126, 134–6, 143
sexual intercourse 32–3, 39, 70, 73, 83, 115, 124
shadowy female 61, 89–90, 132
side-wound 41, 109–10; *see also* wound
Sierra Leone 27–31, 33, 40, 82, 116, 123–5, 127–31, 135, 148
Sifting Time 6, 32, 41–2, 88, 107–8, 146
sin 16, 21, 26, 41, 52, 64, 67, 69–70, 90–1, 101
slavery 26, 86, 111, 121–3, 125, 134, 149–51
Socinians 15
The Song of Los 91, 133–4, 139, 145
Songs of Experience 51, 53–4, 56, 70–1, 73–5
Songs of Innocence 25, 28, 49, 53–5, 60, 70–1, 73–4, 114, 123
Songs of Innocence and of Experience 49, 73, 138
Southey, Robert 31, 113–14, 125–6, 129, 147
Spangenberg, August Gottlieb 35–7
spectre 57, 61, 100–4
Staatskirche 49; *see also* bischöflischer Kirche; Church of England; Episcopal Church; state church
state church 12, 24, 33, 51, 65, 75; *see also* bischöflischer Kirche; Church of England; Episcopal Church; Staatskirche
Stedman, John Gabriel 122, 149
Stoke Newington 16

subscriber (to the belief of Swedenborg) 46–7, 118–20; *see also* delegate
Susquehanna River 125–6
Swedenborg, Emmanuel 5, 8, 20–33, 37, 39, 46–50, 52–3, 66, 76–7, 94, 119–21, 123, 127–30, 134, 137, 143, 147, 150
Swedenborgianism 5–9, 11–13, 18, 20–33, 34, 39, 43, 46–52, 54, 65–7, 69–70, 76–8, 82, 85–6, 88, 93, 111, 116, 118, 120–31, 133–9, 142–4, 148

Tayler, Irene 3–4
Tharmas 63, 96
Theotormon 80, 86–7, 130, 134
Thirty Years War 36
Thirty-Nine Articles 11–12, 40
Thompson, E.P. 5, 7–8, 11, 13–14, 142

Ulro 57
Unitarianism 8, 11–12, 14–20, 21–2, 34, 39–40, 126, 142
Unitas Fratrum 36–7; *see also* Moravian Brethren
Universal Society 120
Urizen 18, 54, 60, 63, 81, 87, 91–2, 96, 132–3, 135
Urthona 60–1, 63, 88, 93, 97, 132
utopia 1, 3–4, 8, 17, 19, 26, 29, 31, 40, 59, 63–4, 79, 81, 94–9, 118, 121, 123–6, 128–30, 134, 139, 145, 147

vagina 39, 41, 52, 73, 75–6, 83, 87, 99, 115
Vala (character) 56, 59–60, 89, 93–4, 96
Vindication of the Rights of Woman 78, 801, 142, 149–51, 154
vision 2, 4–5, 8, 22–5, 27, 47, 49, 57, 63–6, 68, 81, 89, 102, 115, 120–21, 125, 132, 145, 147
"A Vision of the Last Judgment" 65–6
Visions of the Daughters of Albion 39, 71, 73, 78, 80–2, 85–91, 122, 130–2, 135, 149–50
von Breda, Carl Fredrik 27, 123

Wadström, Carl Bernard 27–30, 32, 119–25, 127–30, 143, 147–50
Walkeringham 5
Wesley, Charles 37–8
Wesley, John 37–8, 40
Wollstonecraft, Mary 2–3, 8, 14, 16–18, 20, 39, 78–81, 94, 112, 115–16, 134, 142, 147, 149–51
woman 3, 16, 29–30, 32–3, 43, 45, 58, 62, 64, 66, 68, 70, 75, 77, 80–1, 83, 85, 90–1, 94–5, 104, 106, 115–16, 121–2, 124, 127, 134, 144, 146–7, 149, 151

Index

Wordsworth, William 146
Worrall, David 27–8, 119, 121–27, 130, 138, 147–9, 151
wound 26, 41–3, 108–9, 111; *see also* side-wound
Wright, Catherine *see* Blake, Catherine

Yorkshire 37

Zinzendorf, Count Nicholas Louis 6, 20, 31, 34–7, 39, 42, 44, 107, 143–4, 146
zoa 93–7, 100

www.ingramcontent.com/pod-product-compliance
Lightning Source LLC
Chambersburg PA
CBHW032105300426
44116CB00007B/888